Letter of James

Discipleship Lessons on Practical Christianity

by Dr. Ralph F. Wilson
Director, Joyful Heart Renewal Ministries

JesusWalk® Bible Study Series

Additional books, and reprint licenses are available at:
www.jesuswalk.com/books/james.htm

Free Participant Guide handout sheets are available at:
www.jesuswalk.com/james/james-lesson-handouts.pdf

JesusWalk® Publications
Loomis, California

Paperback

ISBN-13: 978-0-9847340-3-0

ISBN-10: 0984734031

Library of Congress Control Number: 2012900863

Library of Congress subject heading:

    Bible. N.T. James

Suggested Classifications:

    Dewey Decimal System: 227.9

    Library of Congress: BS 2785

Published by JesusWalk® Publications, P.O. Box 565, Loomis, CA 95650-0565, USA.

JesusWalk is a registered trademark and Joyful Heart is a trademark of Joyful Heart Renewal Ministries.

Unless otherwise noted, all the Bible verses quoted are from the New International Version (International Bible Society, 1973, 1978), used by permission.

120117

Preface

James was a practical man. He had seen hypocrisy – in himself, in the Pharisees, in everyday Christians – and he would have none of it. His letter to the early Christian churches is practical and convicting. He talks about heart Christianity worked out in actions. He discusses love and then insists that Christian love can't just speak compassionate words to the hungry – love must feed them.

James was Jesus' younger brother, growing up in the same household. During Jesus' ministry, James had been a skeptic. During Jesus' ministry, James had been a skeptic. After Christ's resurrection, however, he believed and became the lead pastor of the Church at Jerusalem, helping to set the tone for the emerging Christian movement.

Martin Luther called James' Letter "a right strawy epistle" since it didn't present salvation by grace as clearly as in Paul's letters. But I've found it to be a right convicting epistle. James has a way of slicing through all my rationalizations and defenses, and speaking to my heart with power.

May God use this study to help you grow as an authentic disciple with a life patterned after James' brother and Master, Jesus Christ the Lord.

Dr. Ralph F. Wilson
Loomis, California
January 1, 2005

Table of Contents

Reprint Guidelines

Copying the Handouts. In some cases, small groups or Sunday school classes would like to use these notes to study this material. That's great. An appendix provides copies of handouts designed for classes and small groups. There is no charge whatsoever to print out as many copies of the handouts as you need for participants.

All charts and notes are copyrighted and must bear the line:

"Copyright © 2005, 2012, Ralph F. Wilson. All rights reserved. Reprinted by permission."

You may not resell these notes to other groups or individuals outside your congregation. You may, however, charge people in your group enough to cover your copying costs. Free Participant Guide handout sheets are available at:

www.jesuswalk.com/james/james-lesson-handouts.pdf

Copying the book (or the majority of it) in your congregation or group, you are requested to purchase a reprint license for each book. A Reprint License, $2.50 for each copy, is available for purchase at

www.jesuswalk.com/books/james.htm

Or you may send a check to:

Dr. Ralph F. Wilson
JesusWalk Publications
PO Box 565
Loomis, CA 95650, USA

The Scripture says,

"The laborer is worthy of his hire" (Luke 10:7) and "Anyone who receives instruction in the word must share all good things with his instructor" (Galatians 6:6).

However, if you are from a third world country or an area where it is difficult to transmit money, please make a small contribution instead to help the poor in your community.

Introduction to the Letter of James

The Letter of James is one of those no-nonsense New Testament books. James tells it like it is with no holds barred. He doesn't seem concerned that he'll offend someone. He just says it. I've found that the Letter of James is a great place in which to mine and refine practical Christian living.

General Epistle

The Epistle of James is included among the "General" or "Catholic" epistles, since the exact recipient church is not specified. Rather, it seems to have a more general audience, a letter to the whole Church. It is addressed "to the twelve tribes scattered among the nations." The term "twelve tribes" is reminiscent of the 12 tribes of Israel, but it is pretty clear he isn't addressing primarily Jews, but followers of Jesus. So the "twelve tribes" are more figurative, and the expression seems to view the believers as a kind of New Israel and a New Diaspora in the world.

Authorship

Some in the early church felt that the Letter of James was pseudepigraphic, that is, the ascription of a false name of an author to the work.

While early church historian Eusebius (c. 263 - c. 339) regarded the Epistle as canonical (that is, as authoritative Scripture), he says,

> "The first of the Epistles styled Catholic is said to be by James the Lord's brother; but it ought to be known that it is held by some to be spurious. Certainly not too many ancient writers have mentioned it."

Jerome (c. 348 - c. 420), great translator of the Latin Vulgate Bible, wrote:

> "James, who is called the Lord's brother, wrote one Epistle only, which is one of the seven catholic Epistles, which, it is asserted, was published under his name by another, although little by little as time went on it obtained authority."

Ultimately, the Church came to accept the Epistle not only as apostolic, but also that it should be attributed to James, brother of Jesus Christ (Matthew 13:55; Mark 6:3; Galatians 1:19) and the head of the early church at Jerusalem. James apparently became a believer as a direct result of the resurrection of Christ: "he appeared to Peter, and then to the Twelve... Then he appeared to James, then to all the apostles..." (1 Corinthians 15:5, 7). This James was one of the only apostles that Paul met soon after his conversion

(Galatians 1:19), and figured prominently in the Jerusalem Council outlined in Acts 15. He was referred to by Hegesippus (c. 180) as "James the Just," because of his faithful observance of the Jewish law.

The other prominent James mentioned in the New Testament was the brother of John, one of the sons of Zebedee, and a member of Jesus' inner circle of "Peter, James, and John." However, he was beheaded by Herod Agrippa I in 44 AD (Acts 12:2).

Date of the Epistle

Assuming we accept the Letter's authorship by James the Just, the brother of Jesus, it could have been written any time between 40 and 60 AD, but probably closer to 60 AD.

Luther's Criticism

Martin Luther was a bit hard on James, since the letter didn't fit closely enough to his carefully defined doctrine of *sola fide*, "only faith." James says "faith without works is dead" (2:17, 26), and that was a bit much for the Reformer. He wrote about the Letter:

> "In fine, Saint John's Gospel and his first Epistle, Saint Paul's Epistles, especially those to the Romans, Galatians, Ephesians, and Saint Peter's first Epistle, – these are the books which show thee Christ, and teach thee everything that is needful and blessed for thee to know even though thou never see or hear any other book or doctrine. Therefore is Saint James's Epistle *a right strawy Epistle* in comparison with them, for it has no gospel character to it."[1]

As we study the Letter, we'll see that James' divergence from Paul's salvation by grace doctrine is verbal, but not actual or real. And Luther to the contrary, I've found James a very challenging part of my growth as a disciple. He doesn't allow me to hide behind my profession of faith, deceiving myself. He challenges me to live out my faith in my everyday actions, by a love for the helpless, a controlled tongue, earnest prayer, and a concern for the wandering.

I greatly enjoy and am chastened by the Letter of James. I hope the same for you.

---

[1] From Luther's introduction to the 1522 edition of his German New Testament, Ropes' translation.

References and Abbreviations

Adamson   James Adamson, *The Epistle of James* (NICNT; Eerdmans, 1976)

BAGD   Walter Bauer, F. Wilbur Gingrich, and Frederick W. Danker, *A Greek-English Lexicon of the New Testament and Other Early Christian Literature* (Second Edition; based on a previous English edition by W.F. Arndt and F.W. Gingrich; University of Chicago Press, 1957, 1979).

ISBE   Geoffrey W. Bromiley (general editor), *The International Standard Bible Encyclopedia* (Eerdmans, 1979-1988; fully revised from the 1915 edition)

KJV   King James Version (1611)

Merriam-   *Merriam-Webster's Collegiate Dictionary* (Tenth Edition; Merriam-Webster, Webster   1993)

NASB   *New American Standard Bible* (The Lockman Foundation, 1960, 1962, 1963, 1968, 1971)

NIDNTT   Colin Brown (general editor), *The New International Dictionary of New Testament Theology* (Zondervan, 1975-1978; translated with additions and revisions from *Theologisches Begriffslexikon zum Neuen Testament*, 1967-1971, three volume edition)

NIV   New International Version (International Bible Society, 1973, 1978)

NRSV   New Revised Standard Version Bible (Division of Christian Education of the National Council of Churches of Christ in the USA, 1989)

RSV   Revised Standard Version of the Bible (Division of Christian Education of the National Council of Churches of Christ in the USA, 1946, 1952)

TDNT   Gerhard Kittel and Gerhard Friedrich (editors), Geoffrey W. Bromiley (translator and editor), *Theological Dictionary of the New Testament* (Eerdmans, 1964-1976; translated from *Theologisches Wörterbuch zum Neuen Testament*, ten volume edition)

Thayer   Joseph Henry Thayer, *Greek-English Lexicon of the New Testament* (Associated Publishers and Authors, n.d., reprinted from 1889 edition)

1. Experiencing Joy in Trials (1:1-18)

Imagine, if you can, a drill sergeant barking out to green trainees, "when you're ambushed and they start shooting at you, a grin is gonna break across your face, and you're gonna get real happy."

You'd think he was crazy ... and he might be.

But essentially, that's the same thing James is saying in our passage. "Consider it pure joy, my brothers, whenever you face trials of many kinds..." (verse 2). Why should we have joy in our trials? To understand this, we need to understand the value of trials, the nature of trials, and our source of help in these trials. I'm going to consider these questions in a slightly different order than in our text, so bear with me.

The Value of Trials (1:2-4)

"2 Consider it pure joy, my brothers, whenever you face trials of many kinds, 3 because you know that the testing of your faith develops perseverance. 4 Perseverance must finish its work so that you may be mature and complete, not lacking anything." (1:2-4)

James says, "Consider it pure joy ... when you face trials ... because you know that the testing of your faith develops perseverance" (1:3). In other words, we should have joy in knowing that our trials are doing some good. They are building in us a "hang in there" attitude, one which will continue on and not give up.

The word translated "trials" (NIV, NASB, RSV) or "temptations" (KJV) is the Greek word *peirasmos*, "test, trial." But the same word is also used for "temptation, enticement to sin,"[1] thus causing a bit of confusion that James clears up in verse 13. James refers to trials "of many kinds." These may be adverse circumstances such as being hurt by a loved one, or bereavement, poverty, or oppression. Or these trials may be much more diabolical: actual temptation or overt seduction by Satan to sin, such as Jesus experienced (Matthew 4:1-11). As we've learned the hard way, trials and temptations come in all sorts of shapes and sizes. James tells us to let these be a stimulus to joy in our lives.

When we are brand new Christians we have genuine faith, sure enough, but our faith is innocent, untried. As faith is tried, it deepens and matures, and is able to flourish in all sorts of circumstances. And as we know God's faithfulness in various places of testing, we develop the boldness of faith that only a tried and tested faith can possess.

---

[1] *Peirasmos*, BAGD 640-641.

Early in the twentieth century, when people volunteered to become members of the Communist Party in countries like the US or England, new recruits were given a stack of *Daily Worker* newspapers, and instructed to sell them on the street corner, and not return until the papers were sold. Imagine the kind of insults and abuse these green communists were subjected to. Those who continued as members of the Party did so with a commitment that had counted the cost. They were in it for the long haul. Count it all joy, says James, because trials create perseverance in you.

The word variously translated "perseverance" (NIV), "steadfastness" (RSV), "endurance" (NASB), and "patience" (KJV) is the Greek word *hypomonē*, "patience, endurance, fortitude, steadfastness, perseverance."[2] The verb means "to remain behind, stand one's ground, survive, remain steadfast, persevere and also to wait."[3] Trials and temptations build a maturity and completeness in us.

> "Perseverance must finish its work so that you may be mature (*teleios*) and complete (*holoklēros*), not lacking anything." (1:4)

The Greek word *teleios* means "having attained the end or purpose, complete, perfect." When used of people, it means "full grown, mature, adult" or "'perfect, fully developed' in a moral sense."[4] *Teleios* is used here with a another word, *holoklēros*, a qualitative term, which means, "with integrity, whole, complete, undamaged, intact, blameless."[5]

I've met some people, and so have you, who are trying to live as adults with a tiny Sunday School faith. They haven't grown. God intends our trials to make us complete and mature, to build integrity and wholeness in us. Have you let your trials do that? They are to complete us, so we are "not lacking anything."

Q1. (1:2-4) What value have trials had in your life? Have you let Satan destroy you with those trials? Or allowed God to refine you? How have you changed?
http://www.joyfulheart.com/forums/index.php?act=ST&f=64&t=271

Crown of Life (1:12)

Now we're going to skip forward for a moment to verse 12.

[2] *Hypomonē*, BAGD 846.
[3] Ulrich Falkenroth and Colin Brown, "Patience," NIDNTT 2:772-776.
[4] *Teleios*, BAGD 809.
[5] *Holoklēros*, BAGD 564.

> "Blessed is the man who perseveres under trial, because when he has stood the test, he will receive the crown of life that God has promised to those who love him." (1:12)

There is a promise that comes along with our trials, and that is "the crown of life that God has promised to those who love him" (1:12). Our trials set us back. We struggle, we complain to God sometimes, and sometimes we just grit our teeth and hang on. But we do so with the vision ahead of a reward, a promise, a laurel wreath given to the winners, those who have "stood the test." That promise stimulates and encourages perseverance in us.

And so as we grow in the Christian life, we move from innocent, infant faith, yet untried, to faith that is tested and found true, to a confidence in God that enables us to be "more than victors" (Romans 8:37) and laugh with joy at our trials, knowing that God's love for us endures, and that we look forward to a crown of life. This crown is not a reward for extra service, above and beyond the call of duty. It is the crown that consists of eternal life itself. We *have* that life now; we look forward to the words at the end of our journey, "Well done, good and faithful servant, enter into the joy of your Lord," the joy of life in his immediate presence forever.

The Nature of Temptations (1:13-15)

We have examined the *value* of trials. Now let's consider the *nature* of those trials.

> "13 When tempted, no one should say, "God is tempting me." For God cannot be tempted by evil, nor does he tempt anyone; 14 but each one is tempted when, by his own evil desire, he is dragged away and enticed. 15 Then, after desire has conceived, it gives birth to sin; and sin, when it is full-grown, gives birth to death." (1:13-15).

When we get into trouble, it seems like two questions tumble out of our mouths: "What did I ever do to deserve this?" and "Why is God doing this to me?" God *allows* evil in the world – that's part of him allowing us our free will. Did God *create* evil? No. He created the possibility for evil, but that is not the same as creating evil. Let's rephrase that statement. Does God create injustice and unrighteousness? Of course not! He stands diametrically opposed to injustice and unrighteousness, to evil of all kinds.

James applies this by asserting that God does not tempt (*peirazō*) us with evil in order to see if we will fall. It is with this negative sense of "to tempt with evil" that James asserts, "no one should say, 'God is tempting (*peirazō*) me.'" In the same way, Jesus taught his disciples to pray, "Lead us not into temptation (*peirasmos*), but deliver us from evil" (Matthew 6:13). God tests us to strengthen and confirm us in our faith, but the evil in our struggles doesn't come from God – he can't be tempted by evil and never tempts with evil himself.

Q2. (1:13-15) Why do people blame God for evil? Does God tempt us with evil? Does he tempt sinful people with evil? Why does he allow people to sin? Why does he allow evil to exist at all?

http://www.joyfulheart.com/forums/index.php?act=ST&f=64&t=272

Evil Inside (1:14)

The source of the evil is something inside us. "Each one is tempted when, by his own evil desire, he is dragged away and enticed" (1:14). We don't like this sort of teaching, of course. We want to believe that man is basically good and that evil is an aberration, not inherent in man. But the Bible seems to indicate the opposite.

> "And God saw that the wickedness of man was great in the earth, and that every imagination of the thoughts of his heart was only evil continually." (Genesis 6:5)

> "The heart is deceitful above all things, and desperately wicked: who can know it?" (Jeremiah 17:9, KJV)

> "For out of the heart come evil thoughts, murder, adultery, sexual immorality, theft, false testimony, slander. These are what make a man 'unclean'; but eating with unwashed hands does not make him 'unclean.'" (Matthew 15:19-20)

> "... We have already made the charge that Jews and Gentiles alike are all under sin. As it is written: 'There is no one righteous, not even one....'" (Romans 3:9-10, quoting Psalm 14:3)

These verses and others are at the root of what is known as the doctrine of original sin. As St. Augustine expressed it, all men inherit natural corruption from Adam. God created man in his own image (Genesis 1:27) and declared his creation "very good." But Adam and Eve sinned, and they and their offspring "fell" from the original goodness in which God created them. Only Jesus was without sin (Hebrews 4:15). Only he could say, "... The prince of this world cometh, and hath nothing in me" (John 14:30, KJV). Our sins create "footholds" for the devil (Ephesians 4:27), but in Christ there was no foothold of the evil one. Only a single-minded love for his Father.

The Inner Battle

Though there are many evidences of God's good creation, yet this fallenness or depravity extends to every part of man's nature. When we receive Christ as Savior and Lord, there is a desire for God in the inner person, but at the same time a war is raging within us. St. Paul wrote,

"For what I do is not the good I want to do; no, the evil I do not want to do – this I keep on doing." (Romans 7:19)

It is the life of the Spirit within us that delivers us from the power of the sin within us (Romans 8:1-17). But this is a gradual process, called in theological terms, "sanctification."

"Now the Lord is the Spirit, and where the Spirit of the Lord is, there is freedom. And we, who with unveiled faces all reflect the Lord's glory, are *being transformed* into his likeness with ever-increasing glory, which comes from the Lord, who is the Spirit." (2 Corinthians 3:17-18)

"... until we all reach unity in the faith and in the knowledge of the Son of God and become mature, attaining to the whole measure of the fullness of Christ." (Ephesians 4:13)

"Through these he has given us his very great and precious promises, so that through them you may participate in the divine nature and escape the corruption in the world caused by evil desires." (2 Peter 1:4)

"If we confess our sins, he is faithful and just and will forgive us our sins and purify us from all unrighteousness." (1 John 1:9)

Double-Mindedness (1:5-11)

"⁵If any of you lacks wisdom, he should ask God, who gives generously to all without finding fault, and it will be given to him. ⁶ But when he asks, he must believe and not doubt, because he who doubts is like a wave of the sea, blown and tossed by the wind. ⁷ That man should not think he will receive anything from the Lord; ⁸he is a double-minded man, unstable in all he does.

⁹ The brother in humble circumstances ought to take pride in his high position. ¹⁰ But the one who is rich should take pride in his low position, because he will pass away like a wild flower. ¹¹ For the sun rises with scorching heat and withers the plant; its blossom falls and its beauty is destroyed. In the same way, the rich man will fade away even while he goes about his business." (1:5-11)

James introduces two powerful ideas into his letter:

1. We are tempted by the evil desires that remain within us (1:14), and

2. Double-mindedness keeps us from receiving God's wisdom and strength (1:7)

"Double-minded" translates the Greek word *dipsychos*, "doubting, hesitating," literally "double-minded."[6] Until we come to the place where we are willing to face up

---

[6] *Dipsychos*, BAGD 201.

to the sins that hang on in our lives, we continue to experience the inner war that St. Paul alluded to. Until we surrender our evil desires to God and let him work on them, we are "patsies" for sin's temptations.

But trials have a way of forcing the issue, of making "push come to shove." When we have no other place to wriggle out of, in our extremity God helps us identify those parts of our character that are sinful and wrong. We are able to identify those unsurrendered desires that Satan entices and lead us into sin. And at those times, he grants us the ability to repent and see the hold of those sins break and lose their power. Unless we come through these difficult testing times, we don't sort out our priorities and become single-minded in our love for God. Our faith remains stunted and crippled by our double-mindedness, and we remain spiritual babies.

So, in a real way, we can often look back on our trials with pure joy, since it is in those times that God is able to get our attention, help us make new commitments, and embark in new directions.

Q3. (1:5-8) How do trials help cure us of "doublemindedness"? How do trials help us grow in faith?
http://www.joyfulheart.com/forums/index.php?act=ST&f=64&t=273

The Unchangeable Father (1:16-17)

> "16Don't be deceived, my dear brothers. 17Every good and perfect gift is from above, coming down from the Father of the heavenly lights, who does not change like shifting shadows." (1:16-17)

No, God's testings don't lead us to sin. He allows testing in order to *deliver* us from sin. The temptation comes from the evil desires that are within us. Instead, God sends us "good and perfect gifts."

Notice how God is described in verse 17. "The Father of the heavenly lights," an interesting phrase that indicates his role as the Creator of the universe. He is the Light of lights. Next, we see a phrase which indicates that God does not change. The KJV puts it very literally:

> "... with whom is no variableness, neither shadow of turning."

"Variableness" (KJV), "variation" (NASB, NRSV), or "change" (NIV) is translated from the Greek word *parallagē*, "change, variation."[7] This is a rare word, used only here in the New Testament. It is used in Greek for the setting of teeth in a saw, or for stones set alternately, for a sequence of beacons or seasons.[8] "Shadow of turning" refers to the variation in shadows when an object is turned in relationship to a light source. The point is that God the Father does not change nor vary. He is immutable.

This probably doesn't seem to make much difference until you consider what happens when you teach, as do the Latter-Day Saints, that God changes, that he was once a human being who progressed to godhood. This passage teaches clearly and unequivocally that God does not change.

The reason, of course, that James mentions this is that he is making the point that God is committed to "good and perfect" gifts (1:17), not temptation to evil (1:13). God is seeking our good and our perfecting, not our failure or downfall.

Ask God for Wisdom (1:5)

Now that we've understood the value of trials, let's go back to verses 5-8 to understand our need for wisdom.

> "⁵If any of you lacks wisdom, he should ask God, who gives generously to all without finding fault, and it will be given to him. ⁶But when he asks, he must believe and not doubt, because he who doubts is like a wave of the sea, blown and tossed by the wind. ⁷That man should not think he will receive anything from the Lord; ⁸he is a double-minded man, unstable in all he does." (1:5-8)

And what are we to do when we are pressed to the wall and our sins and weaknesses lie exposed? We ask God for wisdom.

> "If any of you lacks wisdom, he should ask God, who gives generously to all without finding fault, and it will be given to him." (1:5)

When we ask people for wisdom, we often hear judgment instead: "I told you so." But not with God. And we have a very clear promise: "It will be given to him."

There is a condition to the promise, however. We must ask with a clear commitment and faith. Unless we deal with our mixed motives and sins, we won't be able to *hear* wisdom even if God speaks to us. Coming to God without repenting of and forsaking the sin that divides our allegiances won't work, either. Adversity and trial have a way of clarifying the issues and highlighting the decisions we need to make. Faith flourishes

---

[7] *Parallagē*, BAGD 620.
[8] Adamson 74.

where we come to a place of a single mind about the things of God, a place where doubt and indecision do not disable action, but where clear, single-mindedness enables it.

Q4. (1:5-8) What is the promise to claim in verse 5? What is the condition attached to this promise in verse 6? How do trials help us receive this wisdom?
http://www.joyfulheart.com/forums/index.php?act=ST&f=64&t=274

He Chose to Give Us Birth (1:18)

The passage closes with a wonder-filled statement of God's grace and mercy towards us, despite our bent to sinning:

> "He chose to give us birth through the word of truth, that we might be a kind of firstfruits of all he created." (1:18)

James speaks of the new birth we have received from God. We'll consider this passage more fully in Lesson 2.

But the point is clear, my friend. God has chosen to give *you* birth. He knows about *your* struggles and sin. They are no surprise to him. Your sins are why Jesus died. Jesus bore your sins on the cross and redeemed you. And your trials and temptations have meaning. They are leading you towards God's wholeness within.

You are his choice. He has life for you, and a plan – to be a firstfruits, a harbinger, a herald of a new age. God himself chose to give *you* birth. What a wonder!

Prayer

Father, thank you for your patience in refining me through my trials. Thank you for helping me really know you better now. Continue to have mercy on me as I grow. In Jesus' name, I pray. Amen.

Key Verses

> "Consider it pure joy, my brothers, whenever you face trials of many kinds." (James 1:2)

> "If any of you lacks wisdom, he should ask God, who gives generously to all without finding fault, and it will be given to him." (James 1:5)

> "Every good and perfect gift is from above, coming down from the Father of the heavenly lights, who does not change like shifting shadows." (James 1:17)

2. Hearing and Practicing the Word (1:18-27)

The theme of this passage centers on God's living Word:

- Being born through the Word (1:18)
- Preferring the Word to moral filth (1:19-21)
- Letting the Word save us (1:21)
- Listening to and practicing the Word (1:22-25)
- Experiencing the freedom of the Word (1:25)
- Living out the Word's teaching in practical ways (1:26-27)

James' readers struggled with the same problem that all of us do. They equated listening to the Word taught in church with living out its implications in their everyday life. We can see this in self-righteous church-goers, but can we see it in ourselves? Probably not, unless God helps us to get very honest. Perhaps in this passage he will do so.

Let's look at each section of this passage in turn.

Being Born through the Word (1:18)

"He chose to give us birth through the word of truth, that we might be a kind of firstfruits of all he created." (1:18)

Though many Bible translations group verse 18 with the previous passage, the more I look at it, the more I see that it introduces and leads into James' teaching on the Word, and probably belongs more closely with 1:19-27.

The phrase "word of truth" appears five times in the English Bible:

"Do not snatch the **word of truth** from my mouth,
for I have put my hope in your laws." (Psalm 119:43)

"And you also were included in Christ when you heard the **word of truth**, the gospel of your salvation. Having believed, you were marked in him with a seal, the promised Holy Spirit...." (Ephesians 1:13)

"... the faith and love that spring from the hope that is stored up for you in heaven and that you have already heard about in the **word of truth**, the gospel...." (Colossians 1:5)

"Do your best to present yourself to God as one approved, a workman who does not need to be ashamed and who correctly handles the **word of truth**." (2 Timothy 2:15)

The fifth time it appears is in our passage:

> "He chose to give us birth through the **word of truth**, that we might be a kind of firstfruits of all he created." (1:18)

First, this passage tell us that we did not appear by chance, but he chose (*boulomai*) to beget us. Our spiritual birth was an act of *his* will first and foremost, and only after that, *our* will.

Second, we read that the *means* of our begetting was "the word of truth." How does a person become spiritually alive? Jesus had discussed this matter with Nicodemus, a well-educated, pious Jew, who later became his disciple. "You *must* be born again," Jesus insisted (John 3:7). In our era, the phrase "born again" is often used in an entirely secular sense to mean renewed or revived or reconstituted, and the religious experience of the new birth is made fun of. But Jesus is completely serious in this conversation. "Flesh gives birth to flesh, but Spirit gives birth to spirit." All of us were born physically, "of the flesh," but according to Jesus, not all have been born spiritually, since this is a requirement to even see or perceive the kingdom of God (John 3:3).

What is the mechanism? I don't claim any absolute insight here. But I believe that the Word begets faith which begets (or maybe *is*) spiritual life. Paul observed, "Faith comes from hearing the message, and the message is heard through the word of Christ" (Romans 10:17, NIV). We see the element of faith, too, in the classic passage on salvation by grace:

> "For it is by grace you have been saved, though faith – and this not from yourselves, it is the gift of God – not by works, so that no one can boast. For we are God's workmanship, created in Christ Jesus to do good works, which God prepared in advance for us to do." (Ephesians 2:8-10)

Paul makes it very clear that the work is all God's, that we are "his workmanship," that this is "not from yourselves, it is the gift of God." So do we even have a part in salvation, or is it all God's work? Theologians have debated this for centuries, the Calvinists versus the Arminians, and we won't solve the riddle here. I conclude that we have only God to thank for our salvation, but that our faith in the Word has an important part still. Paul says we are reconciled to God and presented holy "if you continue in your faith" (Colossians 1:23). Faith in what? Faith in the Word of truth. We "through faith are shielded by God's power until the coming of the salvation that is ready to be revealed in the last time" (1 Peter 1:5). The Word of truth guards and shields this spiritual life, as well.

Third, James touches on the *purpose* of this spiritual birth: "to be a kind of firstfruits of all he has created" (1:18). The word translated "firstfruits" is Greek *aparchē*, a "sacrificial technical term, 'first-fruits' of any kind (including animals, both domesticated and wild), which were holy to the divinity and were consecrated before the rest could be put to secular use."[1] For examples, see Exodus 22:29; Leviticus 2:12-16; Numbers 18:12; Deuteronomy 18:4; 2 Chronicles 31:5; Nehemiah 10:35-39. Firstfruits were the first of the harvest, the first of the crop that was holy and was offered to God at the beginning of the harvest. I don't know the extent of James' meaning. Was he speaking chronologically, as if he and his generation were the firstfruits? Was the rest of the harvest, all Christians up until now? Or is there something beyond that? We can only speculate.

Why do we treasure the Bible? Not because we are superstitious, but because we treasure God's life-giving Word, and that Word is contained within the Bible. It is our anchor, our authority by which to test God's contemporary words, for God has not stopped speaking to his people. "The word of truth" begets new life today if we will but speak it unashamedly!

Q1. (1:18) In what sense are we given spiritual birth by the "word of truth"? What does spiritual life have to do with the Word?
http://www.joyfulheart.com/forums/index.php?act=ST&f=64&t=275

Preferring the Word to Moral Filth (1:19-21)

"[19] My dear brothers, take note of this: Everyone should be quick to listen, slow to speak and slow to become angry, [20] for man's anger does not bring about the righteous life that God desires. [21] Therefore, get rid of all moral filth and the evil that is so prevalent and humbly accept the word planted in you, which can save you." (1:19-21)

Now James turns to the counterfeits and substitutes for the word:

• Man's angry, self-righteous words, and

• Moral filth and evil that would capture our minds and hearts.

We all struggle with anger. Some have it under better outward control than others, to be sure. But anger can pollute us with bitterness, even if we do not lash out openly.

We're angry when we feel wronged. Sometimes it is our selfish pride that has been stepped on. Sometimes it is a violation of our human rights. Sometimes it is even a

---

[1] *Aparchē*, BAGD 81.

desecration of all we hold sacred. Nevertheless, James warns, "Man's anger does not bring about the righteous life that God desires" (1:20). Lest we be quick to think of our anger as moral outrage and righteous indignation, we need to be careful that we do not operate in anger, since the anger does not bring about a righteous life. Yes, anger is to arouse us to action. That is the Creator's intent for giving us anger, I am sure. But once aroused, we must slow down and listen to God concerning what to do, since we cannot *act* in anger and do right.

As we'll see later, I think James had trouble with his own tongue (see 3:2) and knew a lot about this first hand. He begins verse 19, "My dear brothers...." Affectionately. Then he gives the principle he has learned all too well: "Everyone should be quick to listen, slow to speak and slow to become angry." We would do well to memorize this passage. I printed out this verse in large letters and posted it on my bulletin board to remind me not to interrupt my wife when I was angry. "Quick to listen, slow to speak, slow to become angry." I've needed that word. You may need it, too.

Then James says, "Get rid of all moral filth and the evil that is so prevalent" (1:21). KJV has a quaint translation: "Lay apart all filthiness and superfluity of naughtiness...." The word translated "filth" is Greek *rhyparia,* "dirt, filth." Figuratively, in the ethical field, "moral uncleanness, vulgarity," especially, "sordid avarice, greediness."[2] The word translated "evil" (KJV "naughtiness") is *kakia*, a very common word for evil, modified by another common Greek word *perisseia*, "abundance, surplus."[3] Have you ever marveled at the evil around you? There's evil everywhere! Of one type and another, some blatant, some subtle, all deadly. Recognize it, says James, and put it aside.

We are to replace this moral evil with "the word planted in you" (NIV), "the engrafted word" (KJV) that is able to save your souls (*psychē*). This word "engrafted" is a compound word in Greek, *emphytos*, "implanted, engrafted," from *en*, "in, into" and *phyteuō*, "to plant." It is wonderful to ponder. What does it mean that God has given you a "Word-implant"? He has put his thoughts and words deep within you. He has made them part of you. Not only has he put within you a hunger for his Word and his Words, he has given you the precious and tender plant to grow within.

My wife runs a small tree nursery. Every year she purchases hundreds of tree seedlings and plants them in pots. Then she tends and waters them, nurturing them until they become strong and can put down their roots in the soil. The plants are tender and very susceptible to heat and drought until they become established.

---

[2] *Rhyparia,* BAGD 738.
[3] *Perisseia,* BAGD 650.

Letting the Word Save Us (1:21)

> "Therefore, get rid of all moral filth and the evil that is so prevalent and humbly accept the word planted in you, which can save you." (1:21)

Yes, God's words are whispered in our soul by the Holy Spirit and they are within. But we can block them. We can stop our ears by our moral compromise and pride. James says we are to put these all away, and "with humility" accept this word planted deep within us. Peter thinks of it as "imperishable seed:"

> "For you have been born again, not of perishable seed, but of imperishable, through the living and enduring word of God." (1 Peter 1:23)

We can so easily let the clamor and glamour of the world drown out the Word. For Elijah, God was not in the whirlwind, nor in the fire, but in "a still, small voice" (KJV, 1 Kings 19:12; NIV "a gentle whisper"). Are you humble enough to hear it? Are you quiet enough to hear it? Man's words, even man's angry words, are not worth much with regard to spiritual things. It is God's Word that begets us (1:18), God's Word that indwells us (1:21). We would do well to humbly receive it and so save our souls from the destruction of the world.

How are we saved by the Word? Peter puts it this way: "He has given us his very great and precious promises, so that through them you may participate in the divine nature and escape the corruption in the world caused by evil desires" (2 Peter 1:4). We must choose between the filth around us or God's Word. By choosing God's Word, we choose Life.

Listening to and Practicing the Word (1:22)

But now James introduces a serious concern for all Christians, especially those who are constantly in church: "Do not merely listen to the word, and so deceive yourselves. Do what it says" (1:22).

One of the occupational hazards of being a pastor is over-familiarity with God's Word (see 3:1). I read and study and teach it, and have for more than 30 years. But familiarity with the Word, knowing what is right, can be deceiving. It can breed a kind of self-righteousness, a spiritual smugness within us. *We* know the truth. *We* know what is right. But it is quite possible to confuse *knowing* the truth with *doing* it.

Some of the Pharisees in Jesus' day were like that. They were experts in interpreting the Old Testament. And they made an outward show of their observance. But Jesus blasted them as hypocrites. On the outside they looked like clean cups, but inside they were filthy.

> "Woe to you, teachers of the law and Pharisees, you hypocrites! You clean the outside of the cup and dish, but inside they are full of greed and self-indulgence. Blind Pharisee! First clean the inside of the cup and dish, and then the outside also will be clean. " (Matthew 23:25-26)

But before you point your finger at your pastor or the Pharisees, look at yourself. You may have half a dozen Bibles in your home, and that very "Christian-ness" can lull you into an attitude of self-satisfaction. Unless you *practice* God's commands, you kid yourself.

For example, God's Word teaches us, "Be quick to listen, slow to speak, and slow to become angry" (1:19). Do you practice this? Would your spouse or family say you practice this? Knowing it is not enough. Knowing without practicing is self-deceptive.

Q2. (1:22) Why are we so easily fooled into thinking that *listening* to Bible teaching means that we are living out righteous lives? What is the nature of the self-deception? http://www.joyfulheart.com/forums/index.php?act=ST&f=64&t=276

Forgetting What the Mirror Shows (1:23-24)

Now James gives an example to illustrate his point. Listening without doing, he says, is like looking at yourself in the mirror and then immediately forgetting what you look like.

> "23 Anyone who listens to the word but does not do what it says is like a man who looks at his face in a mirror 24 and, after looking at himself, goes away and immediately forgets what he looks like. 25 But the man who looks intently into the perfect law that gives freedom, and continues to do this, not forgetting what he has heard, but doing it–he will be blessed in what he does." (1:23-25)

Though he doesn't quite say it explicitly, James suggests that God's Word is a mirror for the soul that can show us what we really are.

Experiencing the Freedom of the Word (1:25)

He goes on in verse 25:

> "But the man who looks intently into the perfect law that gives freedom, and continues to do this, not forgetting what he has heard, but doing it – he will be blessed in what he does." (1:25)

Twice in James' Letter we find the phrase "the perfect law that gives freedom" (1:25) and "the law that gives freedom" (2:12). It is a strange phrase for a Jew who was called "James the Just" because he kept the Jewish Law. What did he mean by it? How does the Law bring liberty?

It is important to note that James led the Council of Jerusalem in Acts 15 to conclude that keeping the ceremonial law, such as circumcision, was not obligatory for Gentile believers (Acts 15:19-21). This decision was made in place of the position of some Christian Pharisees who contended that "The Gentiles must be circumcised and required to obey the law of Moses" (Acts 15:5). So the "perfect law" is not the Mosaic Law, at least in its entirety.

Rather this perfect law is what James calls the "Royal Law" in 2:8, that is, "Love your neighbor as yourself" (quoting Leviticus 19:18). It is perfect because it sums up, as Jesus had taught, "all the law and the prophets" (Matthew 22:40). It is one of the two great commandments proclaimed by King Jesus: "My command is this: Love each other as I have loved you" (John 15:12).

How liberating this is! Now we no longer live in adherence to a written code, but from the love that God has placed within us, as a natural outflowing of our lives given for others. It is the perfect law *and* the liberating law. And it fulfills the prophecy of Jeremiah that says:

> "The time is coming," declares the Lord,
> "when I will make a new covenant
> with the house of Israel
> and with the house of Judah.
> It will not be like the covenant
> I made with their forefathers
> when I took them by the hand
> to lead them out of Egypt,
> because they broke my covenant,
> though I was a husband to them,"
> declares the Lord.
>
> "This is the covenant I will make with the house of Israel
> after that time," declares the Lord.
> **"I will put my law in their minds
> and write it on their hearts.**
> I will be their God,
> and they will be my people.

No longer will a man teach his neighbor,
or a man his brother, saying, 'Know the Lord,'
because they will all know me,
from the least of them to the greatest,"
declares the Lord.
"For I will forgive their wickedness
and will remember their sins no more." (Jeremiah 31:31-34)

James exhorts us to look intently into this perfect law of liberty (1:25) and so never forget who God is, and who we are, and how he wants us to love and live.

Q3. What is this "perfect law" that James mentions? How would you define it? How does it relate to the "royal law" (2:8)? In what sense does it bring liberty?
http://www.joyfulheart.com/forums/index.php?act=ST&f=64&t=277

Living Out the Word's Teaching in Practical Ways (1:26-27)

"26If anyone considers himself religious and yet does not keep a tight rein on his tongue, he deceives himself and his religion is worthless. 27Religion that God our Father accepts as pure and faultless is this: to look after orphans and widows in their distress and to keep oneself from being polluted by the world." (1:26-27)

This perfect, liberating law of love, then, governs what James considers pure religion. Sometimes Evangelical Christians are offended by the use of the word "religion"; they much prefer a more specific word, such as "Christianity" or "Christian faith."

But here in verses 26-27, James uses a general word for religion, both an adjective and a noun. The noun is Greek *thrēskeia*, "the worship of God, religion," especially as it expresses itself in "religious service" or "cult." The adjective is *thrēskos*, "religious."[4] James isn't trying to put other religions on a par with Christianity. But he is asserting that if we would consider ourselves authentic worshippers of God, then we must live out this liberating law of love in our everyday lives.

James mentions three tests of pure religion:

1. A tongue that is kept under control (1:26)
2. Looking after orphans and widows (1:27a), and
3. Keeping oneself from being polluted by the world (1:27b).

---

[4] *Thrēskos*, BAGD 363.

We'll look further at the tamed tongue, since James expounds on it at greater length in chapter 3. I find it curious, however, that he selects caring for orphans and widows as one of the tests of true religion. The reason, I am sure, is that orphans and widows have no power or money to benefit us. Therefore, when we care for their needs it is a truly unselfish act, and one surely motivated by love.

Do you see caring for the poor and needy as too demeaning? Too dirty for your refined sensibilities? Then you may be in danger, James would say, of being selfish rather than loving. Instead of the Word changing your heart, other forces control you. Again and again in Scripture we see that God cares for the poor. Perhaps the classic verse is:

> "Circumcise your hearts, therefore, and do not be stiff-necked any longer. For the Lord your God is God of gods and Lord of lords, the great God, mighty and awesome, who shows no partiality and accepts no bribes. He defends the cause of the fatherless and the widow, and loves the alien, giving him food and clothing. And you are to love those who are aliens, for you yourselves were aliens in Egypt." (Deuteronomy 10:16-19)

If God defends the cause of the orphan and widow and gives them food and clothing, who are we to be too pure to aid those who are poor? We're so concerned that the person who holds up a sign saying "Will Work for Food" is trying to take advantage of us, that we end up closing our heart to him. Would you rather be "taken" by the poor a few times and be generous in your heart? Or protect yourself from ever being deceived, but have a stingy and unloving heart?

The passage in Deuteronomy also indicates that God loves the alien. This might offend us, but I am sure he loves the *illegal* alien, too. That doesn't mean that we shouldn't control our borders. But what it does mean is that we are to love those who are sojourning in our country just as God loves them. Our first question should be not "Do they have a green card?" Our first question should be, "Do they have enough to eat?"

This is the sign of a person whose religion is "pure and faultless." How does my practice measure up to the Perfect Law? How does yours?

Q4. (1:26-27) Why does James make taming the tongue and caring for the poor the prime tests of pure religion? Why not the quality of our quiet time or worship?
http://www.joyfulheart.com/forums/index.php?act=ST&f=64&t=278

Spiritual Pollution (1:27b)

> "Religion that God our Father accepts as pure and faultless is this: ... to keep oneself from being polluted by the world." (1:27b)

The final characteristic of pure religion is "keeping oneself from being polluted by the world." The Greek word translated "polluted" (NIV) or "spotted" (KJV) is Greek *aspilos*, "spotless, without blemish."[5] It comes from the verb *spiloō*, "stain, defile."[6]

I was eating a garden-fresh tomato the other day, and some of it fell on the shirt I was wearing. If I ignore the spill and let it dry, it can easily set in the cloth fibers and become a permanent stain. So I take off the shirt, put soap on the tomato spot, wash it thoroughly in the basin, and then rinse it. I think I washed out the spot before it stained. I hope!

James says that keeping from being stained by the anti-God world's standards and pollutions and greed and sensuality – this is part of true religion. Character, someone said, is what we do when no one is looking. If we let spots from the world set in our lives and hearts, they can and do become permanent stains on our character.

We must watch our hearts lest they become stained with cynicism and unbelief, bitterness and unforgiveness. "Keep thy heart with all diligence; for out of it are the issues of life" (Proverbs 4:23, KJV).

There is a sense in Scripture where we are to cleanse ourselves. Later in this Letter, James exhorts us, "Come near to God and he will come near to you. Wash your hands, you sinners, and purify your hearts, you double-minded" (4:8). We see a similar theme in the Book of Revelation: "These are they who have come out of the great tribulation; they have washed their robes and made them white in the blood of the Lamb" (Revelation 7:14). Christians are to take sin seriously and approach it with repentance and sorrow, and all earnestness.

But in another sense, we are powerless to cleanse ourselves. So we must humbly confess our sins to the One who has promised to both "forgive us our sins *and* purify us from all unrighteousness" (1 John 1:9).

Hearing the Living Word and Doing It

The Letter of James is so challenging because he doesn't ask us primarily what we *believe* about Jesus. He asks us what we are *doing* because we have encountered him. He doesn't allow us to hide behind our church-going and Bible reading, our "hearing" of the Word. He calls us to be doers to the Word, as well.

---

[5] *Aspilos*, BAGD 117.
[6] *Spiloō*, BAGD 762.

There have been times when I have deceived myself in the midst of my Christianity. May God grant that I will do this no more. But that I will peer intently into the mirror of the Perfect Law of Liberty – and remember – and do it.

Prayer

Lord, we ask you to help us to turn our hearts back to you. Strip away our self-deception. Convict us of our sins. Expel our excuses. And help us humble ourselves before you. In Jesus' name, we pray. Amen.

Key Verses

"My dear brothers, take note of this: Everyone should be quick to listen, slow to speak and slow to become angry, [20]for man's anger does not bring about the righteous life that God desires." (James 1:19-20)

"Do not merely listen to the word, and so deceive yourselves. Do what it says." (James 1:22)

"Religion that God our Father accepts as pure and faultless is this: to look after orphans and widows in their distress and to keep oneself from being polluted by the world." (James 1:27)

3. Forsaking Favoritism for Love (2:1-13)

Think back.

You have been the object of partiality. Perhaps your mother or father liked you more. Or your teacher or your employer. Because of your special relationship with a superior, you got promotions when another was just as qualified. Or perhaps you have never been the favored one.

You have also been the object of discrimination. Perhaps it was for how you looked – your height, your weight, your complexion, your hair. Perhaps you've experienced discrimination on the basis of your intelligence, your race, your religion, your gender. Your family's social standing in the community has been a factor, either negative or positive, on how you were viewed by the elite. How did it make you feel?

You may be bearing the scars of those encounters to this very day. It is this huge – and is the central issue that James tackles in these passages.

Partiality in the Church (2:1-3)

"[1] My brothers, as believers in our glorious Lord Jesus Christ, don't show favoritism. [2] Suppose a man comes into your meeting wearing a gold ring and fine clothes, and a poor man in shabby clothes also comes in. [3] If you show special attention to the man wearing fine clothes and say, 'Here's a good seat for you,' but say to the poor man, 'You stand there' or 'Sit on the floor by my feet,' [4] have you not discriminated among yourselves and become judges with evil thoughts?" (2:1-4)

You'd think that the church would be a place where class falls away and we are all equal as children at the feet of Jesus. Unfortunately, it wasn't so in New Testament days and it isn't so in our own. James calls on us to recognize the problem and deal with it.

James, leader of the Jerusalem church, had probably seen it in the gatherings of that great Mother Church. A rich person enters and all the elders are kowtowing to him, falling over themselves to honor him with attention, with flattery, with the best seat in the house. Perhaps he'll become a regular part of the church and be able to give big offerings, they think. Sound familiar?

Then a poor man enters on a day when all the seats are filled. His clothing needs mending and he hasn't taken a bath for a while. Stand there, we tell him. There are some seats on the floor at the front, that's all we can offer, we tell him, hoping that he'll find somewhere else to go to church. His presence is an embarrassment. Too many poor people and we'll be thought of as a poor-person's church. It will reflect on us. And they'll expect us to give them things. Sound familiar?

Definitions

The word translated "favoritism" (NIV), "personal favoritism" (NASB), "respect of persons" (KJV), or "partiality" (RSV) is the Greek word *prosōpolēmpsia* – "partiality."[1] It is used elsewhere in Romans 2:11; Ephesians 6:9; Colossians 3:25; Acts 10:34 (masculine noun); James 2:9 (verb form). The word is derived from a Hellenistic compounding of two words: *prosōpon* ("face") and *lambanō* (I.4. 'to take,' i.e. 'to admit, receive'), that is, to accept a person you know or favor.[2]

A look at our English word "partial" fills out the meaning: "1. of or relating to a part rather than the whole; not general or total. 2. inclined to favor one party more than the other, biased. 3. markedly fond of someone or something."[3]

We have three other English words that describe this behavior.

1. **Bias** "bent, tendency; an inclination of temperament or outlook, especially a personal and sometimes unreasoned judgment, prejudice."[4]

2. **Discrimination**, "the act, practice, or an instance of discriminating categorically rather than individually; prejudiced or prejudicial outlook, action, or treatment."[5]

3. **Prejudice**, from the words "pre" + "judge": preconceived judgment or opinion; an adverse opinion or leaning formed without just grounds or before sufficient knowledge; an irrational attitude of hostility directed against an individual, a group, a race, or their supposed characteristics."[6]

When I read those definitions, I think about some of my own knee-jerk reactions to the homeless and to certain other groups. James calls it what it is: sin.

Q1. (2:1-3) What kind of person or what kind of sinner do you tend to discriminate against? What kind of people are you (or your church) trying to make a good impression on?

http://www.joyfulheart.com/forums/index.php?act=ST&f=64&t=279

---

[1] *Prosōpolēmpsia*, BAGD 720.

[2] *Prosōpolēmpsia*, Thayer 550.

[3] *Merriam Webster Collegiate Dictionary*, 10th edition, p. 847.

[4] *Ibid.*, p. 110.

[5] *Ibid.*, p. 332.

[6] *Ibid.*, p. 119.

Judges with Selfish and Evil Motives (2:4)

James asks, "Have you not discriminated (*diakrino*) among yourselves and become judges with evil thoughts?" (2:4). What is the source of the evil? In a word, selfishness.

We treat the rich with solicitude and honor since they have power and wealth, and we hope that by our actions some of that honor and power and wealth might rub off on us. It never hurts to be on the good side of a rich person, you know. Our actions are selfish, self-serving. As Paul said,

> "For the love of money is a root of all kinds of evil. Some people, eager for money, have wandered from the faith and pierced themselves with many griefs" (1 Timothy 6:10).

Our discrimination is based on our own love of money.

And how about our mistreatment of the poor? Selfish again. We don't want to be pulled down to their level, either social or economic, and don't want to feel obligated to help them. Selfishness, love of money.

Churches are hardly immune from this behavior. It may not be the rich that are fawned over; it may be young married adults with growing families who are perceived as the prize. Single moms and the elderly are tolerated, but often not openly welcomed or courted by calls or visits. We're trying to grow a church, we tell ourselves, and these people form a good social and economic base that allows us to do this. But in the meantime we are guilty of prejudging the poor and the elderly and the divorced. We sin because we look to our own needs and not to theirs.

Q2. (2:4) In what way does favoritism make one a judge? How does favoritism make one a judge with "evil thoughts"?
http://www.joyfulheart.com/forums/index.php?act=ST&f=64&t=280

Poor and Rich in God's Kingdom (2:5-7; 1:9-11)

> "5 Listen, my dear brothers: Has not God chosen those who are poor in the eyes of the world to be rich in faith and to inherit the kingdom he promised those who love him? 6 But you have insulted the poor. Is it not the rich who are exploiting you? Are they not the ones who are dragging you into court? 7 Are they not the ones who are slandering the noble name of him to whom you belong?" (2:5-7)

> "1:9 The brother in humble circumstances ought to take pride in his high position. 10 But the one who is rich should take pride in his low position, because he will pass away like a wild flower. 11 For the sun rises with scorching heat and withers the plant; its blossom

falls and its beauty is destroyed. In the same way, the rich man will fade away even while he goes about his business." (1:9-11)

When you look at this brief Letter of James, you can see that James is stirred up about the subject of the favor shown to the rich. In 2:5-7 he is ironic: aren't the rich the very people who exploit you and try to cheat you in court?

The first few verses of chapter 5 also indict the rich for hoarding their wealth, cheating the poor, living in luxury and self-indulgence, and climbing over the bodies of the innocent poor in order to do so (5:1-6). Those of us who live middle class lives in America are richer than the rich of James' day ever were. What about us?

James' congregation struggled with poverty. Once during a famine, Paul had to raise an offering to help the poor in Jerusalem (1 Corinthians 16:1; 2 Corinthians 8:19-20; Acts 24:17). James is careful to help the poor to value themselves as God values them.

> "The brother in humble circumstances ought to take pride in his high position." (1:9)

> "Has not God chosen those who are poor in the eyes of the world to be rich in faith and to inherit the kingdom he promised those who love him?" (2:5)

While the rich seem to have everything in this life, such a view is superficial, says James. Looking with eternal eyes, with Kingdom eyes, we see that the rich will fade away (1:11) and find all their hoarded wealth rotted and corroded (5:2-3). Instead of honor, the rich who have gained their wealth unrighteously will face a judgment of fire (5:3).

These are hard words. But so much of the time *we ourselves* see with worldly, materialistic eyes. And this blindness to eternal things feeds our partiality and prejudice. We must take off our blinders and see with new eyes, God's eyes.

The Royal Law, the King's Law (2:8)

> "If you really keep the royal law found in Scripture, "Love your neighbor as yourself," you are doing right." (2:8)

Our King, Jesus, offered us a different perspective, a different law: "Love your neighbor as yourself" (Leviticus 19:18).

> "Hearing that Jesus had silenced the Sadducees, the Pharisees got together. One of them, an expert in the law, tested him with this question: 'Teacher, which is the greatest commandment in the Law?'
> "Jesus replied: '"Love the Lord your God with all your heart and with all your soul and with all your mind." This is the first and greatest commandment. And the second is like it: "Love your neighbor as yourself." All the Law and the Prophets hang on these two commandments.'" (Matthew 22:34-40)

"A new command I give you: Love one another. As I have loved you, so you must love one another. By this all men will know that you are my disciples, if you love one another." (John 13:34-35)

The center of Jesus' ministry was love – love for the poor, love for those rejected by society, love for the sick. He didn't come for himself, he came for them. For us.

"For even the Son of Man did not come to be served, but to serve, and to give his life as a ransom for many." (Mark 10:45)

"For God so loved the world that he gave his one and only Son, that whoever believes in him shall not perish but have eternal life." (John 3:16)

Partiality and prejudice and favoritism are essentially self-serving, self-centered. Our King, on the other hand, was essentially self-giving and centered on the needs of others. The Law that governed his life is what his brother James calls the Royal Law: "Love your neighbor as yourself." (1:8)

Self-Centered Lawbreakers (2:9-11)

"9But if you show favoritism, you sin and are convicted by the law as lawbreakers. 10For whoever keeps the whole law and yet stumbles at just one point is guilty of breaking all of it. 11For he who said, 'Do not commit adultery,' also said, 'Do not murder.' If you do not commit adultery but do commit murder, you have become a lawbreaker." (2:9-11)

But while the Royal Law of love states it most clearly, it is not unique. Rather it capsulizes and condenses the spirit of the whole Mosaic Law. For example, we read:

"The same law applies to the native-born and to the alien living among you." (Exodus 12:49)

"You are to have the same law for the alien and the native-born. I am the Lord your God. " (Leviticus 24:22)

"One and the same law applies to everyone who sins unintentionally, whether he is a native-born Israelite or an alien." (Numbers 15:29)

Again and again the Israelites are warned to show justice and care towards the poor of the land:

"Do not pervert justice; do not show partiality to the poor or favoritism to the great, but judge your neighbor fairly." (Leviticus 19:15)

"There will always be poor people in the land. Therefore I command you to be open-handed toward your brothers and toward the poor and needy in your land." (Deuteronomy 15:11)

The scripture also warns us against injustice in the system, systemic evil:

"If you see the poor oppressed in a district, and justice and rights denied, do not be surprised at such things; for one official is eyed by a higher one, and over them both are others higher still." (Ecclesiastes 5:8)

The point is that if we are so concerned about keeping laws, we need to heed the clear laws about partiality in the Bible. "If you show favoritism you sin and are convicted by the law as lawbreakers" (2:9).

Verses 10 and 11 underscore the point. "Whoever keeps the whole law and yet stumbles at just one point is guilty of breaking all of it" (2:10). We cannot be selective in our observance of Jesus' commands. We can't say: I'm such a righteous person, God will overlook this one tiny area. No, we must accept partiality and prejudice as sins, and repent of them. They are evil in God's sight. We cannot hide behind our excuses.

Q3. (2:9-11) Why does James refer to the Great Commandment as the "Royal Law"? How is it more "royal" than the Mosaic Law? How does showing favoritism toward a rich person break the "Royal Law" towards that rich person? How does it break the "Royal Law" in regard to a poor person?
http://www.joyfulheart.com/forums/index.php?act=ST&f=64&t=281

The Law that Liberates (2:12)

"Speak and act as those who are going to be judged by the law that gives freedom...." (2:12)

In verse 12 is a wonderful expression, "the law that gives freedom" (NIV) or "law of liberty" (KJV, RSV, NASB). James uses a similar expression in 1:25 "the perfect law of liberty." Just what does he mean? The phrase "law of liberty" is almost an oxymoron. Most laws restrict and set limits. But the King's Law liberates and frees. David Hubbard put it this way:

"Anger and hatred are not freedom. They tie us in knots; they goad us to say and do things we do not really believe in. Love is liberating because it trusts God to be the final judge and encourages us to do good wherever we can."[7]

At its core, this Law that Liberates is not a written code, but the Spirit of God working in our hearts and writing God's ways and words on our hearts. This way our actions begin to spring from a changed heart rather than from a well-trained set of conditioned responses. In a word, we are liberated.

---

[7] David Hubbard, *The Book of James: Wisdom that Works* (Word, 1980), p. 39.

But more than that, we liberate those whom we used to judge. Where we used to show favoritism to our cronies and discriminate against others, now by this Royal Law of Love we liberate the outcasts of society. We show them love and this energizes in them the potential to be all *they* can be, too. By our love-actions we liberate both our own selves and we liberate our society.

Mercy Triumphs Over Judgment (2:13)

"… Because judgment without mercy will be shown to anyone who has not been merciful. Mercy triumphs over judgment!" (2:13)

In our favoritism, we cannot set ourselves up as judges, because at best we are "judges with evil thoughts" (2:4), and we will be judged ourselves. If we don't show mercy, we will not receive mercy. Jesus said that we will be judged by the same measures of judgment we use to judge others (Matthew 7.2).

Rather, we can show *mercy*. We can let the Royal Law that has liberated our own spirits give another chance to others who have struggled under sin and selfishness. If we judge those people we also judge ourselves. We were there, too. But Christ now, by his mercy, has set us free.

Yes, God is just and will exercise just judgment. We are assured of that throughout the Bible, and especially in the Book of Revelation. But while he is just, he is also loving. He loves to show mercy. In fact, he delights in it.

This causes a serious problem. How can you both be completely *just* like God is, and, at the same time, be overflowing with *love and mercy*? Doesn't that make you schizophrenic? This is how God solved it.

Jesus came to give us life and model before us the Father's love. Then he, in his own body, became the ransom for our sins. He took our sins upon himself and became an atonement for our sins, the Greater for the lesser.

"He himself bore our sins in his body on the tree … by his wounds you have been healed." (1 Peter 2:24)

"For God so loved the world that he gave his only begotten Son, that whosoever believes in Him should not perish, but have everlasting life." (John 3:16)

And so God is both just – he punished our sin upon His own Son who took our sins upon him – and loving, now he forgives our sins freely, mercifully.

It's an old story and a simple one. One by one, God has helped people to understand this simple but profound truth. "This is a faithful saying," said the Apostle Paul, who in his youth had persecuted Christians unto death, "and worthy of all acceptance, that

Christ Jesus came into the world to save sinners; of whom I am chief" (1 Timothy 1:15). How can we *not* show mercy, when we are so dependent upon it ourselves?

And so this section of James' Letter concludes with the words, "Mercy triumphs over judgment" (2:13). The word translated "triumph over" (NIV, RSV, NASB) or "rejoice against" (KJV) is Greek *katakauchaomai*, "boast against, exult over; triumph over."[8]

It is our bragging point as believers. Not that God will send people to hell for their sins. He will, but he takes no delight in it. Our bragging point is that our God shows mercy to sinners, and delights to do so. Let us tell the world.

Q4. (2:13b) In what way is showing regard towards the wealthy (2:2-3) a denial of mercy? *Extra credit*: **Read Hosea 6:6; Matthew 5:7; and 9:13. In what way does mercy "triumph over" (NIV, RSV, NASB) or "rejoice against" (KJV) judgment? What does this mean?**
http://www.joyfulheart.com/forums/index.php?act=ST&f=64&t=282

Prayer

Lord, forgive me of my selfish, self-serving partiality in the way I treat and think about people. Help me to love – really love! – the least and poorest in society. Help me to delight in showing mercy – just as you do. In Jesus' name, I pray. Amen.

Key Verses

"If you really keep the royal law found in Scripture, "Love your neighbor as yourself," you are doing right. But if you show favoritism, you sin and are convicted by the law as lawbreakers." (James 2:8-9)

"Mercy triumphs over judgment!" (James 2:13b)

---

[8] *Katakauchaomai*, BAGD 411.

4. Energizing Your Faith by Works (2:14-26)

Some years ago I began a business newsletter that reaches nearly 100,000 readers each week. I don't use it to preach the gospel, but rather as a place of witness. In one issue, I remember God guiding me to include a brief verse that I thought was apt to my readership of business entrepreneurs. This is all I said, at the very end of the newsletter:

> "Finally, a word for Web marketers who want to make lots of money (others please disregard): 'Remember the Lord your God, for it is he who gives you the ability to produce wealth....'" (Deuteronomy 8:18)

That's it. Nothing more. But I got an angry response from a reader:

> "In your issue 12 of *Web Marketing Today* you drop a bible quote. This offends me. I have my own religious beliefs which I consider a personal matter. I respect the views of others, but I resent having them impose their views upon me. If you intend to use your business newsletter as a religious soapbox then you will be losing at least this reader, and probably many more. Don't jeopardize an otherwise good project by mixing business and religion." – John D.

This is the way I answered him in the next issue. I quoted his letter, and then said:

> "John, I hardly intend *WMT* as a soapbox for religion. But I strongly believe that if we business people don't mix our religion and ethics into our businesses we harm ourselves, our businesses, *and* our nation. If a single Bible verse offends you, so be it. My faith is part of who I am, and will naturally be part of how I communicate." – Ralph F. Wilson, Editor

I got dozens and dozens of e-mail notes from Christians over the next few days saying, "Thank you for what you said!" That experience taught me a great deal. There will always be people who try to push us Christians into fearful silence. But we must never let them do this. We must let our religion mix with our business and real life. Because unless we do, our faith is dead.

Bare Faith (2:14-18)

James tackles an issue that must have been prominent in his day, that of silent believers, of inactive believers, people who might have difficulty in court assembling enough evidence to prove they were Christians.

Essentially James is asking, "Can faith exist by itself, unconnected from the rest of one's life?" And his answer is a resounding. No way! Faith without deeds is a dead faith!

"Faith by itself, if it is not accompanied by action, is dead" (2:17).

It may have the appearance of the real thing. The person may even view himself or herself as a Christian, since they've gone to church and heard the Word, and know all the right things to do and say. But that can be extremely deceptive:

"Do not merely listen to the word, and so deceive yourselves. Do what it says" (1:22).

For several years when I was in my late twenties, I worked on a research project at the California Institute of Technology in Pasadena. The goal was to extract DNA and RNA from various stages of fresh peas and pea plants, and then compare the differences in the controlled environment of the lab. I would grind up fresh peas, for example, and gradually purify the DNA until it became long strands that I could wrap around a glass rod. Once it had been the "brains" of pea cells, driving all their activities. Now it was pure, separated from all the messy pea stuff it had once intimately known. But it was also dead. Yes, we could perform experiments on it and watch it coil and uncoil and bond with RNA. But it was no longer living.

Faith is like that. Separated from life and spun into the long strands of theological theory, it may represent true orthodoxy in its belief system, but it is sterile. Faith, as James speaks about it, is *not* a system of belief, but a way of life that consciously draws its sustenance from God and lives for God and is energized by God himself. The word "dead" here and in 2:26 is the Greek adjective *nekros*, "dead, without life."

Q1. (2:14-18) In what sense is faith dead if it is unaccompanied by action? In what sense might (if that were possible) it be alive?
http://www.joyfulheart.com/forums/index.php?act=ST&f=64&t=283

Feeding the Poor (2:15-16)

James forces us to look at a practical example.

"Suppose a brother or sister is without clothes and daily food. If one of you says to him, 'Go, I wish you well; keep warm and well fed,' but does nothing about his physical needs, what good is it?" (2:15-16)

What we see here is not faith in action, but selfishness. Faith is active. Faith motivates us. Faith makes a difference. If we trust in the Living God, we can't stand by and mouth positive platitudes in the face of the poor. We must help warm and feed them.

"In the same way," James says, "faith by itself, if it is not accompanied by action, is dead." (2:17)

Q2. (2:15-16) To what degree are we responsible for the poor and needy in the church community? How about our responsibility for those outside the church, in the community at large?

http://www.joyfulheart.com/forums/index.php?act=ST&f=64&t=284

The Faith of Demons (2:18-19)

Now James goes one step further by highlighting the difference between bare intellectual assent and living faith.

> "But someone will say, 'You have faith; I have deeds.'
> Show me your faith without deeds, and I will show you my faith by what I do. You
> believe that there is one God. Good! Even the demons believe that – and shudder" (2:19)

Does a demon believe in the existence of the One God? Of course. He has a pretty acute awareness of spiritual realities. That belief also is frightening to him. He trembles in fear. But does he "believe" in the sense of "have faith"? No.

The Amplified Bible, which can be tediously wordy at times, has a very helpful way of translating the Greek word *pisteuō* – to believe. At John 3:16, for example, they translate, "... whoever believes in (trusts, clings to, relies on) Him...."

In Greek, as in English, the verb "believe" can refer to intellectual assent or conviction, as well as a trust in (in a religious sense). Usually (though not always) the grammatical construction is different.[1] In 2:19 the construction makes clear the idea of intellectual assent to the concept rather than reliance and trust in God.

It is possible, you see, to have faith without love. I have met many people who had impeccable orthodox Christian beliefs, but no real love for God. Their thoughts were in order, but their love was cold. Just like the demons, they believed in the truth, but did not then submit their lives, hearts, and souls to follow the True One.

See how deadly this is? Many Christians that will sit next to you in church this Sunday will believe right things, but have in them no love for God. They may even live a moral life, but their heart has not been changed. It is still self-centered, not God-centered, motivated by self interest rather than love for others. Thus they can say pretty words to their poor Christian church attenders – "I wish you well! Keep warm and well

---

[1] *Pisteuō*, BAGD 660-662. The concept of "believe" in an intellectual sense often has the object of that belief in the accusative, or the object of a preposition such as *hoti* ("that"). On the other hand, the concept of "believe in, trust in" is usually expressed by the dative, or the preposition *eis* ("unto, in"), or *epi* ("upon").

fed!" – but not lift a finger to help them. This kind of faith that has no actions to express it is truly stillborn. It has the shape without the life.

Q3. (2:18-19) What is the difference between the "belief" of a demon and the "belief" of a practicing Christian? The "belief" of a non-practicing Christian?
http://www.joyfulheart.com/forums/index.php?act=ST&f=64&t=285

Potential Faith

A few miles from my home, the mighty Folsom dam stands 340 feet high and holds back the waters of the South and North forks of the American River. When full, the reservoir holds 1,010,000 acre-feet of water. Its powerhouse contains three generators capable of providing 198,720 kilowatts of electrical power, enough electricity to light 2 million 100 watt bulbs per hour – but only when the water is flowing through its turbines.

Folsom Dam. Photo: US Bureau of Reclamation

If all the dam does is hold back water, the stream below the dam dwindles to a trickle and the fish downstream die. The lights dim and flicker off in the City of Roseville because its mighty generators produce no power.

Faith without works is dead in the same way that a dam that only holds back water is useless. The power is generated when the potential is actuated by actions and deeds in real life.

Illustrations from the Scripture (2:20-26)

Now James moves to prove his contention from Scripture that "faith without deeds is useless (KJV 'dead')" (2:20).[2]

---

[2] The last word in the English text of 2:20 is somewhat in dispute regarding what was in the "original" Greek text. The KJV follows the Textus Receptus ("received text") in reading "dead" (*nekra*), supported by many manuscripts Aleph, A, C², K, P, Psi, Byz Lect and some Syriac and Coptic texts. However, the editorial committee of the United Bible Societies' Greek New Testament (3rd edition), felt strongly that the alternate reading "useless, unproductive" (*argē*) was more likely, since it is strongly supported by many

James begins with Abraham offering his son Isaac on the altar (Genesis 22), and argues that Abraham was considered righteous for what he did, for his deed. "You see that his faith and his actions were working together, and his faith was made complete by what he did" (2:22). It is crucial that we understand what James is saying. He is not asserting that Abraham is saved by what he did, but that what he did was an outworking of his faith, and that the two were inseparable, they were "working together" (Greek *synergeō*).

The action fulfilled the scripture, says James, that reads, "Abraham believed God, and it was credited to him as righteousness" (quoting Genesis 15:6). One could argue that this was said about Abraham prior to the incident of offering Isaac on the altar. I don't think James would disagree. Abraham's act of offering Isaac on Mt. Moriah was an outworking of his faith; it complemented and completed it.

The other example James gives of faith and deeds together was Rahab the prostitute hiding the spies in her house in Jericho and then helping them escape their enemies (Joshua 2). I think it's marvelous that James would refer to Rahab as "the prostitute," in light of his concern about "keeping oneself from being polluted by the world" (1:27). Her past is represented by the word "prostitute," but her place in history was secured by having enough faith in the Hebrew's God that she risked her own life to protect and aid God's servants. It is a beautiful example of faith's outworking manifested in action.

James concludes this section: "As the body without the spirit (Greek *pneuma*, "breath") is dead, so faith without deeds is dead" (2:26).

Works verse Grace Controversy

However, Protestants especially struggle with some of the issues that James raises. One of the Apostle Paul's primary themes is to champion salvation by faith, not by works. This is the theme of his Letter to the Galatians, for example:

> "[We Jews] know that a man is not justified by observing the law, but by faith in Jesus Christ. So we, too, have put our faith in Christ Jesus that we may be justified by faith in Christ and not by observing the law, because by observing the law no one will be justified." (Galatians 2:16)

---

manuscripts B, C*, it, Vulgate, some Coptic and Aramaic texts) and may involve a play on words. It is also easy to explain the reading "dead," since it is used several other times in this passage. "Useless" is the "harder" reading but makes good sense in the context and is followed by the NIV, NASB, and RSV "barren". Deciding between alternate readings in the early Greek manuscripts is called the science of Textual Criticism. This one is fairly easy to decide, but the evidence in some texts is pretty evenly divided.

Perhaps the principal of salvation by grace through faith is best summed up in Ephesians 2:8-9:

> "For it is by grace you have been saved, through faith – and this not from yourselves, it is the gift of God – not by works, so that no one can boast."

Without a careful reading one might conclude that James and Paul are in conflict, but they are not. Jewish Christians in Jerusalem faithfully observed the Jewish law *and* celebrated their faith in Christ. Surely, some of James' associates in Jerusalem held very strict views concerning keeping the Jewish Law. James himself was called "James the Just" by Hegesippus for doing so. We read about an incident that took place in the Gentile city of Antioch, where Paul had to rebuke Peter for hypocrisy along this line:

> "Before certain men came from James, [Peter] used to eat with the Gentiles. But when they arrived, he began to draw back and separate himself from the Gentiles because he was afraid of those who belonged to the circumcision group." (Galatians 2:12)

Peter acted one way towards the Gentile Christians when he came to Antioch, but when strict law-keeping Jewish Christians arrived from Jerusalem, Peter felt intimidated and began to act as they did, somewhat superior to the Gentile Christians. Paul felt he needed to take a stand.

> "The other Jews joined [Peter] in his hypocrisy, so that by their hypocrisy even Barnabas was led astray. When I saw that they were not acting in line with the truth of the gospel, I said to Peter in front of them all, 'You are a Jew, yet you live like a Gentile and not like a Jew. How is it, then, that you force Gentiles to follow Jewish customs? We who are Jews by birth and not "Gentile sinners" know that a man is not justified by observing the law, but by faith in Jesus Christ. So we, too, have put our faith in Christ Jesus that we may be justified by faith in Christ and not by observing the law (KJV "works of the law"), because by observing the law (KJV "works of the law") no one will be justified.'" (Galatians 2:13-16)

You see, Paul is combating an early Jewish Christian heresy that contended that it was necessary to observe the Jewish law in order to be saved, such things as submitting to circumcision, keeping the dietary laws, separation from Gentiles, and all the minutiae for which Jesus had criticized the Pharisees.

Paul is strongly against the heresy that one must perform certain Jewish rituals in order to be saved ("works of the law"). But he is not against "good works" that are a natural outflow of our faith and of God's work of redemption and regeneration within us. He concludes his famous "saved by grace through faith ... not of works" passage with these words: "For we are God's workmanship, created in Christ Jesus to do good works, which God prepared in advance for us to do" (Ephesians 2:10). In other words, we are not saved *by* works, but saved *in order to do* good works.

I don't think Paul would have an quarrel with James about this matter. While there seems to be a verbal inconsistency, it comes from the way each is using the word "works." Paul is combating "works of the law" necessary for salvation, but both he and James would agree that "good works" are a natural and inescapable result of a living faith in Christ.

Q4. (2:20-26) How does James' point about the necessity of works jive with Paul's emphasis on salvation by grace without works (Ephesians 2:8-10)?
http://www.joyfulheart.com/forums/index.php?act=ST&f=64&t=286

Luther and the Reformers

Martin Luther was upset at the way in which the Catholic Church in his time seemed to teach that people were saved by acts of piety. This was a distortion of what the Church believed at its core, but no doubt the practice of Catholicism in the towns and villages and parishes needed to be reformed at this point.

So Luther preached Paul's letters with force and fire. He proclaimed that we are saved *sola fide*, only by faith. That observing religious rituals had nothing to do with earning one's salvation, that it was a gift. He saw clearly the message of grace; his words were a much needed corrective to religious practice in his time.

But Luther himself was disappointed in James. He wrote about the Letter:

"In fine, Saint John's Gospel and his first Epistle, Saint Paul's Epistles, especially those to the Romans, Galatians, Ephesians, and Saint Peter's first Epistle, – these are the books which show thee Christ, and teach thee everything that is needful and blessed for thee to know even though thou never see or hear any other book or doctrine. Therefore is Saint James's Epistle *a right strawy Epistle* in comparison with them, for it has no gospel character to it."[3]

I think Luther underrated the Letter of James. True, James' message is not the saving gospel. His calling was more to help existing Christians ("the twelve tribes scattered among the nations") learn how to live consistent, Christian lives and not get hung up with the self-deception that leads to hypocrisy.

---

[3] From Luther's introduction to the 1522 edition of his German New Testament, Ropes' translation.

Paul's theme was salvation as a gift through faith. Luther's theme was only faith. James' theme is that genuine faith always shows itself in deeds. We need to learn from all of these voices, and not underemphasize any.

James calls to us through the centuries: "Faith without works is dead." And he speaks a powerful word to the dead religiosity and self-deception that we need to renounce if we are to live on the cutting edge of faith today. Thanks, James. We needed you.

Prayer

Father, it's easy for us Christians to slip into an intellectual faith that is cold towards the people you love. I've seen this in myself. Forgive me and put me in gear, so that my engine is connected to my wheels once again. In Jesus' name, I pray. Amen.

Key Verses

"Suppose a brother or sister is without clothes and daily food. If one of you says to him, 'Go, I wish you well; keep warm and well fed,' but does nothing about his physical needs, what good is it? In the same way, faith by itself, if it is not accompanied by action, is dead." (James 2:15-17)

"But someone will say, 'You have faith; I have deeds.' Show me your faith without deeds, and I will show you my faith by what I do. You believe that there is one God. Good! Even the demons believe that–and shudder." (James 2:18-19)

5. Attaining Tongue-Taming Wisdom (3:1-18)

Have you ever had to correct a person about a fault that you constantly struggle with yourself? It's tough. It makes you feel like a hypocrite. I think James is having difficulty talking about taming the tongue for the same reason.

The Peril of Teachers (3:1-2)

He begins this section somewhat apologetically:

"Not many of you should presume to be teachers, my brothers, because you know that we who teach will be judged more strictly. We all stumble in many ways. If anyone is never at fault in what he says, he is a perfect man, able to keep his whole body in check." (3:1-2)

Why should teachers be judged more strictly? Because they can't claim, "I didn't know any better." They've been teaching others how to behave; God and everyone else expects them to practice what they preach.

James is humbled by this realization. As I read the Letter of James I get the feeling that James is the kind of person who has strong opinions and a quick tongue. He castigates the rich relentlessly, for example. The Letter is pretty hard hitting; James isn't working to phrase his words diplomatically or so they don't offend. He just says them outright – and I'm sure God wanted him to, so we couldn't miss the point.

But I get the feeling that *because* James was plain-spoken, he also sometimes struggled with controlling his words. Earlier in the letter he had cautioned his readers – notice, with gentleness,

"My dear brothers, take note of this: Everyone should be quick to listen, slow to speak and slow to become angry, for man's anger does not bring about the righteous life that God desires." (1:19-20)

Q1. (3:1-2) Why does James discourage people from aspiring to be teachers of the Word? Why is greater strictness appropriate? Should you set higher standards for your pastor than you do for yourself?
http://www.joyfulheart.com/forums/index.php?act=ST&f=64&t=287

Remedy 1: Bridle the Tongue – Self Control (3:2)

> "We all stumble in many ways. If anyone is never at fault in what he says, he is a perfect man, able to keep his whole body in check." (3:2)

James concedes, "We all stumble in many ways...." (3:2). The word used is difficult to translate in English: "We all stumble in many ways" (NIV, NASB), "in many things we offend all" (KJV), and "we all make many mistakes" (RSV). The Greek word is *ptaiō*, literally, "stumble, trip," then figuratively, "to make a mistake, go astray, sin."[1] The word indicates a trip, rather than a complete fall, as Romans 11:11 indicates.

Then he defines maturity or perfection: "If anyone is never at fault in what he says, he is a perfect man, able to keep his whole body in check (*chalinagōgeō*)" (3:2). This is similar to a statement he made earlier: "If anyone considers himself religious and yet does not keep a tight rein (*chalinagōgeō*) on his tongue, he deceives himself and his religion is worthless" (1:26).

In both verses he uses the Greek verb *chalinagōgeō*, "guide with a bit and bridle, hold in check."[2] Just as a person would be liable for the damage incurred for not restraining a runaway horse, so we must restrain or bridle our tongues. This is the essence of "pure religion." It is a hallmark of the "perfect man" or "mature man" (3:2).

He's talking, of course, about exercising careful self-control, the first remedy for an out-of-control tongue. Later we'll be looking at the second remedy to taming the tongue, but the first element is self-control.

> "Set a guard over my mouth, O Lord;
> keep watch over the door of my lips." (Psalm 141:3)

We are careful to train our children to control what they say. And we can force ourselves to "mind our tongue," even though it's very hard!

Small Cause, Large Effects (3:3-5)

> "[3]When we put bits into the mouths of horses to make them obey us, we can turn the whole animal. [4]Or take ships as an example. Although they are so large and are driven by strong winds, they are steered by a very small rudder wherever the pilot wants to go. [5]Likewise the tongue is a small part of the body, but it makes great boasts. Consider what a great forest is set on fire by a small spark." (3:3-5)

---

[1] *Ptaiō*, BAGD 727.
[2] *Chalinagōgeō*, BAGD 874.

Now James continues with his analogy of bridling. Whereas we differentiate between bits and bridles, the Greek term apparently treats them as a single item: *chalinos*, refers to both a bit *and* bridle.[3] In these verses he gives several examples of small objects with large effects:

- Bit - guide a horse
- Rudder - steer a ship
- Tongue - great boasts
- Spark - start a forest fire

Destructive Power of the Tongue (3:6-8)

"[6]The tongue also is a fire, a world of evil among the parts of the body. It corrupts the whole person, sets the whole course of his life on fire, and is itself set on fire by hell.

[7]All kinds of animals, birds, reptiles and creatures of the sea are being tamed and have been tamed by man, [8]but no man can tame the tongue. It is a restless evil, full of deadly poison." (3:6-8)

His analogy of a spark starting a forest fire leads into his next section about the terrible destructive power of the tongue: "The tongue also is a fire...." (3:6)

The tongue almost takes on its own persona in the next verses. He calls it "a world of evil (Greek *adixia*, "unrighteousness") among the parts of the body." He sees it as a corrupter of the whole person. The word translated "corrupts" (NIV), "staining" (RSV) or "defiles" (NASB, KJV) is Greek *spiloō*, "stain, defile," from the noun *spilos*, "spot," figuratively "stain, blemish."[4] The tongue stains and defiles the body.

This is reminiscent of Jesus' reply to the Pharisees who were so worried about ceremonially dribbling water on their hands before eating food.

"Don't you see that whatever enters the mouth goes into the stomach and then out of the body? But the things that come out of the mouth come from the heart, and these make a man 'unclean.'" (Matthew 15:17-18)

Carrying on the idea of the spark igniting a great fire, James continues that the tongue "sets the whole course of his life on fire" (3:6). You've probably experienced that. One slip, one irretrievable word, and a relationship is ruined, a job is lost, a career is short-circuited. I had a friend who was better than anyone I've ever known at securing work. But he seldom lasted more than a few weeks on any job. He didn't have his temper and

---

[3] *Chalinos,* BAGD 874.
[4] *Spiloō,* BAGD 762.

tongue under control. In one twelve month period I once counted that he obtained – and lost – 14 different jobs. His and his family's lives have been set on fire by his tongue. You have your own set of examples, I'm sure.

Set on Fire by Hell (3:6b)

Finally, James observes that the tongue "is itself set on fire by hell (*gehenna*)" (3:6b). The Greek word *gehenna* is a Greek transliteration of the Hebrew for Valley of Hinnom, the name of a ravine to the south of the city of Jerusalem. Here child sacrifices had been made to the false god Molech. It was written of evil King Ahaz:

> "He burned sacrifices in the Valley of Ben Hinnom and sacrificed his sons in the fire, following the detestable ways of the nations the Lord had driven out before the Israelites." (2 Chronicles 28:3)

"The fire" was identified early with the Valley of Hinnom. It was also a place where the prophets Jeremiah pronounced terrible curses of God's judgment and slaughter of the wicked (Jeremiah 7:31-32; 19:1-6). Isaiah saw the judgment of the wicked in terms of burning: "And they will go out and look upon the dead bodies of those who rebelled against me; their worm will not die, nor will their fire be quenched, and they will be loathsome to all mankind" (Isaiah 66:24). By the second century B.C., the Valley of Hinnom had come to be equated with the hell of the last judgment.[5]

There is some evidence that the Valley of Hinnom was the refuse dump of Jerusalem. The Prophet Jeremiah identifies the location of the Valley of Hinnom as "near the entrance of the Potsherd Gate" (Jeremiah 19:2), that is, the place where broken pots were discarded. New Testament scholar Joachim Jeremias observes, "It was still in modern times the place for rubbish, carrion, and all kinds of refuse."[6] Jeremias also cites an ancient Jewish document that identifies the Dung Gate as leading to the Valley of Hinnom.[7] It is logical, then, that it was a place where garbage burned continually.[8] If Gehenna also has the connotation of burning refuse and garbage and uncleanness, then James' comment, that the tongue "is itself set on fire by Gehenna" is particularly apt.

---

[5] Joachim Jeremias, "*gehenna*," TDNT 1:657-658.

[6] Joachim Jeremias, *Jerusalem in the Time of Jesus* (Fortress Press 1962, translated 1965), p. 17.

[7] Ibid., p. 310.

[8] Both David John Wieand, "Hinnom, Valley of," ISBE 2:717, citing Lightfoot; and Leon Morris, *Matthew* (Eerdmans, 1992), p. 115; see this as a possibility.

The Untamable Tongue (3:7-8)

> "⁷All kinds of animals, birds, reptiles and creatures of the sea are being tamed and have been tamed by man, ⁸but no man can tame the tongue. It is a restless evil, full of deadly poison." (3:7-8)

Now comes the part that James struggles with, that he cannot fully understand. Human beings have been able to tame all kinds of animals, birds, reptiles, and sea creatures, he says but not the tongue. Why is that? A couple sentences later, he is appalled that with the same tongue we both praise God and curse men. It should not be so.

He concludes that the tongue is untamable. He personifies it again, calls it a "restless evil (*akatastaton kakon*), full of deadly poison." "Evil" is the common Greek word *kakos*, "'evil,' what is contrary to law, crime, sin."⁹ The word translated "restless" (NIV, NASB, RSV) or "unruly" (KJV) is *akatastatos*, "unstable, restless,"¹⁰ James uses the same word in 1:8: "he is a double-minded man, *unstable* in all he does."

So the tongue is a fire, a world of evil, a corrupter, an unstable evil, a deadly poison. Untamable. Is there no hope?

Q2. (3:7-8) Read Matthew 12:34 and 15:18. In light of these verses, why is the tongue untamable? What has to happen before it can be tamed?
http://www.joyfulheart.com/forums/index.php?act=ST&f=64&t=288

Out of the Same Mouth (3:9-12)

> "⁹With the tongue we praise our Lord and Father, and with it we curse men, who have been made in God's likeness. ¹⁰Out of the same mouth come praise and cursing. My brothers, this should not be. ¹¹Can both fresh water and salt water flow from the same spring? ¹²My brothers, can a fig tree bear olives, or a grapevine bear figs? Neither can a salt spring produce fresh water." (3:9-12)

Now James struggles with the ugly truth that out of the same mouth come praise and cursing. On the one hand he acknowledges that our mouths do say bad things. On the other he strongly protests and uses several pairs in nature to demonstrate that this is an anomaly:

• Praising God vs. cursing men

⁹ *Kakos*, BAGD 397-398.
¹⁰ *Akatastatos*, BAGD 30.

- Fresh water vs. salt water
- Fig tree vs. olive tree
- Salt spring vs. fresh water

He doesn't resolve the discrepancy. He merely points out its incongruity and then says, "My brothers, this should not be" (verse 10).

Remedy 2: Purify the Heart – An Inner Humility

What we say begins in the heart. Jesus observed, "Out of the overflow of the heart the mouth speaks" (Matthew 12:34). Self-control, "bridling the tongue," as James puts it, is vital. But at best it is only partial. The second remedy for a runaway tongue he suggests is a humble, purified heart. Where the heart has been changed, then the triggers that used to set off our mouths are now disabled and disconnected.

Humility, Envy, and Selfishness (3:13-16)

"13 Who is wise and understanding among you? Let him show it by his good life, by deeds done in the humility that comes from wisdom. 14 But if you harbor bitter envy and selfish ambition in your hearts, do not boast about it or deny the truth. 15 Such 'wisdom' does not come down from heaven but is earthly, unspiritual, of the devil. 16 For where you have envy and selfish ambition, there you find disorder and every evil practice." (3:13-16)

"Who is wise and understanding among you? Let him show it by his good life, by deeds done in the humility that comes from wisdom" (3:13). Here is a repeat of James' theme of faith being demonstrated by works. It is also a preview of the theme of humility and submission to God that forms the core of chapter 4. The key is humility.

Set against humility is "bitter envy and selfish ambition" (3:14). The Greek word *eritheia* in verse 14 is translated as "selfish ambition" (NIV, RSV, NASB) and "strife" (KJV). Before NT times the word is found only rarely, "where it denotes a self-seeking pursuit of political office by unfair means." Bauer, Arndt, and Gingrich conclude that "for Paul and his followers ... the meaning 'strife, contentiousness' [as if the word were derived from *eris*, "strife, discord, contention"] cannot be excluded. But 'selfishness, selfish ambition' in all cases gives a sense that is just as good, and perhaps better."[11]

When we're in the midst of a political season we can get pretty cynical. What kind of person aspires to political office? we wonder. What kind of ego is necessary to put up with all the garbage one must endure to become elected? Is it just raw ambition?

---

[11] *Eritheia*, BAGD p. 309.

First, I don't believe that ambition itself is a bad thing. If we didn't aspire to something better, something higher, no progress at all would be made in society. Ambition is a dogged persistence towards a goal to accomplish something. We are ambitious for our families, to make a better life for them. We are ambitious for noble causes of all kinds. We should be ambitious for God, to see his Kingdom come on earth as it is in heaven. Ambition is essential. Ambition is a good thing.

But second, ambition is too easily entwined with other motivations. We wrap ambitions in our own sense of self-worth, and so achievement of our goals is no longer pure. It is no longer to accomplish lofty goals. It is also to vindicate our own selves, and to highlight our own achievements. And so it becomes selfish, self-serving. Lofty ambitions become convenient blinds from which to further our own objectives of popularity, power, and prosperity.

I don't think we should be cynical just about politicians. We should be distrustful of our own motivations. Why are we working so hard to achieve? How much of this is pure selfish gain? If we would be honest, a good deal of the noble causes we're involved with have selfish tentacles wrapped around our souls feeding the pride, the fear, the lust, the greed that lies within.

And it is just this pride and fear, lust and greed that slip out when we speak. Others often hear it before we do. "Freudian slips," we call them. Our words betray our hearts. So why do we have strife and verbal sparring? Why do we come out with a critical spirit and put-downs of our opponents at work and at home? Because of the selfishness that is in our hearts. James says this kind of so-called "wisdom" is earthly, unspiritual, of the devil" (3:15). It is the root of "disorder and every evil practice" (3:16). Purify your heart, implies James, and you'll tame the tongue.

Q3. (3:13-16) In what ways are "bitter envy" and "selfish ambition" (3:14) direct opposites of "humility" (3:13)? How does denial of "bitter envy" and "selfish ambition" prevent healing? How does boasting about these prevent healing?
http://www.joyfulheart.com/forums/index.php?act=ST&f=64&t=289

Heavenly Wisdom (3:17)

"17 But the wisdom that comes from heaven is first of all pure; then peace-loving, considerate, submissive, full of mercy and good fruit, impartial and sincere. 18 Peacemakers who sow in peace raise a harvest of righteousness." (3:17-18)

We know more than we want to about the "wisdom" that comes from the devil (3:15). In its place James suggests a different kind, "the wisdom that comes from heaven" (3:17).

Look at the words that describe this heavenly wisdom, and then compare it to words from the famous "love chapter" in 1 Corinthians 13.

James 3:17

- Pure
- Peace-loving
- Considerate
- Submissive
- Full of mercy and good fruit
- Impartial
- Sincere

1 Corinthians 13

- Patient
- Kind
- Does not envy
- Does not boast
- Not proud
- Not rude
- Not self-seeking
- Not easily angered
- Keeps no record of wrongs
- Does not delight in evil
- Rejoices with the truth
- Always protects
- Always trusts
- Always hopes
- Always perseveres
- Never fails

Contrast that with bitter envy and selfish ambition and you see that the kind of wisdom James is talking about is love. Taming the tongue requires changing the heart, so that we are no longer filled with selfishness, but selflessness – in a word, love. We can "put a guard on our lips" and exercise self-control, but until love displaces selfishness in our hearts we will still have mouth eruptions. Love never fails.

Q4. (3:17-18) With what tool do peacemakers sow peace? Why does this produce a ripening crop of righteousness? In whom does this crop grow?
http://www.joyfulheart.com/forums/index.php?act=ST&f=64&t=290

Peacemaking Words (3:18)

James concludes with a word about peacemakers: "Peacemakers who sow in peace raise a harvest of righteousness" (3:18) Compare that to Jesus' beatitude: "Blessed are the peacemakers, for they will be called sons of God" (Matthew 5:9).

Peacemakers are people who insert peace in the midst of strife, rather than continue the dispute. Peacemakers are often misunderstood as weak. Jesus certainly was. But the seeds sown in peace bring a harvest of righteousness.

Fighting starts with the flaming tongue of anger, which, James says, "does not bring about the righteous life that God desires." But fighting is put to an end when we speak with the tongue of peaceful, unselfish words, that produces the righteousness that God *does* desire.

Prayer

Lord, work in us so that what we say will consistently honor you. Give us self-discipline, and even more, displace our self-absorption with your out-flowing love. In Jesus' name we pray. Amen.

Key Verse

"Not many of you should presume to be teachers, my brothers, because you know that we who teach will be judged more strictly." (James 3:1)

6. Submitting Yourself to God (4:1-12)

We can be so arrogant and independent towards God! If there's a single obstacle to growing as a disciple of Jesus it is our pride. Not the good kind of self-esteem pride that we need to grow as people. But that variety of "I-can-do-it-myself" pride that we can so easily fall prey to. It all starts in the heart.

Fights and Quarrels (4:1-2)

I expect that as pastor of Christendom's Mother Church at Jerusalem, James had seen all too much bickering and picking and criticizing. This, too, finds its root in pride, and James addresses it in this chapter. Some of the words he uses are:

- **Fights**, Greek *polemos* (4:1) – literally "armed conflict, war, battle, fight," then figuratively "strife, conflict, quarrel."[1]
- **Quarrels**, Greek *machē* (4:1) – "fight, quarrel, dispute."[2]
- **Battle**, Greek *strateuō* (4:1) – "do military service, serve in the army," then figuratively, of the struggles of the passions within the human soul (James 4:1; 1 Peter 2:11)."[3]
- **Kill**, Greek *phoneuō* (4:2) –"murder, kill."[4] Jesus compared unrestrained anger with murder (Matthew 5:21-22), since anger is one of the roots of murder.
- **Covet**, Greek *zeloō* (4:2) – in a bad sense "be filled with jealousy, envy toward someone."[5]
- **Quarrel** (*polemeō*) and **fight** (*machomai*) (4:2). See related words above.

I remember two pretty good tenors in one church I pastored. One was filled with jealousy at the other – who was the better singer – and he couldn't find a kind word to say. Sounds like the "bitter envy and selfish ambition" that James talked about in 3:14. So many church fights that are outwardly about issues, are under the surface are about power ("selfish ambition") and bitter envy. God help us!

---

[1] *Polemos*, BAGD 685.
[2] *Machē*, BAGD 496.
[3] *Strateuō*, BAGD 770.
[4] *Phoneuō*, BAGD 864.
[5] *Zeloō*, BAGD 338.

That isn't to say that churches don't have to work through difficult problems sometimes. They do, just like families. But we need to do it with love and not with spite.

Some years ago, a regional division of my denomination had to disfellowship four local congregations for their stand affirming a homosexual lifestyle. I came back from the meeting proud of my denomination (for a change). In this case, the whole meeting was conducted with respect and care. You could sense grief in the room at the same time the delegates voted to disfellowship these churches. I was both proud that our churches were willing to make a difficult decision, but also that they made the decision in love and in an absence of name-calling. So often it isn't so.

As long as we are on this earth we will have strife and conflict, since we are different people with different points of view. But we must let our love flow in spite of our differences. And we can examine ourselves, and purify ourselves of base motivations.

Hedonism as a Way of Life (4:3)

Twice in the first three verses of chapter four, James uses the Greek word *hedonē*, from which we get our English word "hedonism."

> "What causes fights and quarrels among you? Don't they come from your desires (*hedonē*) that battle within you?" (4:1)

> "When you ask, you do not receive, because you ask with wrong motives, that you may spend what you get on your pleasures (*hedonē*)." (4:3)

In these verses, *hedonē* is variously translated "desires," "lusts," "passions," or "pleasures." It means "pleasure, enjoyment, pleasantness," usually in the bad sense of "(evil) pleasure, lust."[6]

We generally use the word "hedonism" as a kind of synonym for "decadence." But I would guess that at least 50% of the people on the face of the earth live by this unwritten rule:

> "I will choose what seems to offer me the greatest happiness."

Sounds pretty innocent. Everyone wants to be happy. But seeking personal happiness as our main goal in life means – by definition – (1) that we are not living to love others and seek their good when it conflicts with our own, and that (2) we have not surrendered our lives to fulfill God's will for us. Pursuit of personal happiness is selfishness, pure and simple. But it is so common a personal philosophy that we take it for granted.

---

[6] *Hedonē*, BAGD 344.

A great many Christians are more committed to their own personal happiness than they are doing God's will. And that may sometimes include you – and me.

We don't have what we want, James says in verse 2, because we do not ask God. Why is that? Sometimes it is because we are afraid to bring God into our lives too much, since we might not like what he would say. We prefer to go it on our own rather than be obligated to God.

There's an old story about a lady who told her friend about a terrible problem she had, and that now all she could do was pray. "My, my," answered her friend. "Has it come to that?"

> "You do not have, because you do not ask God. When you ask, you do not receive, because you ask with wrong motives (Greek *kakos*), that you may spend what you get on your pleasures." (4:2b-3)

One of the reasons God doesn't give us what we ask for is because of our heart selfishness, literally, "you ask badly or wrongly." Our motivations are wrong. We ask not for a good purpose, but for an evil one, a self-centered one, to spend it (*dapanaō*) on our hedonism. The Greek verb *dapanaō* means "spend, spend freely."[7] It's like asking our Dad for money and then using it to go out and carouse. How long do you think he'll be giving you money if he knows that's what you'll do with it?

Our selfishness, our pleasure-serving, can and does block answers to our prayers.

Q1. (4:1-3) Is God against pleasure? What wrong in living to increase one's pleasure?
http://www.joyfulheart.com/forums/index.php?act=ST&f=64&t=291

Flirting with Spiritual Adultery (4:4)

> "You adulterous people, don't you know that friendship with the world is hatred toward God? Anyone who chooses to be a friend of the world becomes an enemy of God." (4:4)

Now James gets downright personal. Literally, he addresses the pleasure-loving reader as "You adulteress!" You might think that he would use the masculine form of the word, "adulterer" since most of the readers would probably be men. He uses the feminine form deliberately, however, because he is referring to believers as married to God. This is a theme you can trace all the way from the Old Testament (where God's

---

[7] *Dapanaō*, BAGD 171.

people were thought of as God's wife, and he their Husband), to the New Testament (where the Church is considered "the bride of Christ").

> "For your Maker is your husband–
> the Lord Almighty is his name–
> the Holy One of Israel is your Redeemer;
> he is called the God of all the earth." (Isaiah 54:5)

> "I will betroth you to me forever;
> I will betroth you in righteousness and justice,
> in love and compassion.
> I will betroth you in faithfulness,
> and you will acknowledge the Lord." (Hosea 2:19-20)

> "I am jealous for you with a godly jealousy. I promised you to one husband, to Christ, so that I might present you as a pure virgin to him." (2 Corinthians 11:2)

> "Husbands, love your wives, just as Christ loved the church and gave himself up for her.... This is a profound mystery – but I am talking about Christ and the church." (Ephesians 5:25, 32)

> "Let us rejoice and be glad
> and give him glory!
> For the wedding of the Lamb has come,
> and his bride has made herself ready." (Revelation 19:7)

> "One of the seven angels who had the seven bowls full of the seven last plagues came and said to me, 'Come, I will show you the bride, the wife of the Lamb.'" (Revelation 21:9)

> "The Spirit and the bride say, 'Come!' And let him who hears say, 'Come!' Whoever is thirsty, let him come; and whoever wishes, let him take the free gift of the water of life." (Revelation 22:17)

When we are married to one husband, but flirt with another lover, we are adulterous. And that is what we are doing when we cozy up to the world system that doesn't love or follow Jesus Christ. Our love affair with pleasure, our friendliness towards that which grieves God, "is hatred toward God," James says. "Anyone who chooses to be a friend of the world becomes an enemy of God."

Q2. (4:4) Why does James refer to church members as "adulteresses"? What does the adultery consist of? Who is the aggrieved husband? What is wrong with friendship with the world?
http://www.joyfulheart.com/forums/index.php?act=ST&f=64&t=292

Envying Intensely (4:5)

> "Or do you think Scripture says without reason that the spirit he caused to live in us envies intensely?" (4:5)

Verse 5 is difficult to understand with precision. We can't identify the exact passage James is referring to. Certainly envy, jealousy, and ambition afflict man (3:14-16) and corrupt his spirit. On the other hand, the concept of God's jealousy towards his people is a clear theme in the Old and New Testaments, for example, in Genesis 6:3-7; Exodus 20:5; Zechariah 1:14; Matthew 6:24; Romans 8:7; 1 John 2:15-17.

The key Greek words in James 4:5 that the NIV translates "envies intensely" are *phthonon epipothei*. The verb is *epipotheō*, "long for, desire something."[8] The noun is *phthonos*, "envy, jealousy."[9]

There are two alternatives:

1. Some English translations attribute this intense jealousy as God, the jilted husband, toward is bride, his adulterous people, along the lines of the theme of the Old Testament book of Hosea, such as the RSV's "He yearns jealously over the spirit which he has made to dwell in us."

2. Other English translations attribute the envy and jealousy to the corrupt human spirit. The New English Bible translates, "The spirit which God implanted in man turns to envious desires." J.B. Phillips translates, "Do you imagine that this spirit of passionate jealousy is the Spirit he has caused to live in us?"[10] The NIV translates more ambiguously: "Or do you think Scripture says without reason the spirit he caused to live in us envies intensely?"

The alternatives are discussed thoroughly by James Adamson, who translates the verse: "Or do you suppose it is an idle saying in the scriptures that the spirit that has taken its dwelling in us is prone to envious lust?"[11]

However you take this verse, the idea is a conflict between how in his independence man is acting and feeling, and the desires and purposes of his Creator for him.

---

[8] *Epipotheō*, BAGD 298.
[9] *Phthonos*, BAGD 857.
[10] J.B. Phillips, *The New Testament in Modern English* (Macmillan, 1958).
[11] Adamson, *James*, pp. 170-173.

Grace to the Humble (4:6)

> "But he gives us more grace. That is why the Scripture says,
>   'God opposes the proud
>   but gives grace to the humble.'" (4:6, quoting Proverbs 3:34)

"Grace" is a word you'd expect to find the Apostle Paul using. But here it is in James. God's grace helps us in our struggles with sin, in our struggles with the pleasure principle. God's Spirit woos us to him and, as we recognize our sins and humble ourselves in repentance, we receive grace.

It seems that too many conversions these days take place without a deep repentance. There is often a sense of need, an emptiness, answered by a trust in the Lord that fills us with joy and hope. And that is good. But at some point – or points – God needs to humble us so we are willing to turn away from our ingrained sins. Often that requires the pain of self-discovery and finally a heartfelt repentance. It's best when we can fully repent at the beginning of our Christian walk, but often there are some deep humblings as God lovingly strips back layer after layer of selfishness and trains us to be his holy ones, his disciples.

I've struggled with pride in my life. So when I encounter this passage: "God opposes the proud," I find myself distinctly desiring not to set myself up as God's opponent. I don't want to find myself on opposite sides of the ring "duking it out" with God. How about you? Where does your stubbornness (an alternate word for "pride") place you in relation to God?

Submitting Yourself to God (4:7-10)

The next few verses give clear instructions in repentance and – who knows – may arise straight out of a first century Jerusalem Church revival meeting.

> "⁷Submit yourselves, then, to God. Resist the devil, and he will flee from you. ⁸Come near to God and he will come near to you. Wash your hands, you sinners, and purify your hearts, you double-minded. ⁹Grieve, mourn and wail. Change your laughter to mourning and your joy to gloom. ¹⁰Humble yourselves before the Lord, and he will lift you up." (4:7-10)

James takes the words of his quotation from Proverbs 3:34 (resist/oppose, proud/humble) and uses them in an exhortation:

1. "Submit yourselves, then, to God" (4:7a).

Here's the general principle. To "submit oneself" (*hypotassō*) means to come into voluntary obedience to a person, to bend your will to that person's. If you've been proud you need to voluntarily (not only under duress) bend your will to God's will.

2. "Resist the devil, and he will flee from you" (4:7b).

The word "resist" is Greek *anthistēmi*. It means "set against, set oneself against, oppose, resist, withstand."[12] Our problem too often is that we are double-minded, clinging both to our selfish desires *and* a desire to please God. We must clearly take a stand against the devil and at the same time let go of the desire that gives him power over us.

What is the relation between the devil and temptation? Does the devil make you do it? Satan certainly tempted Jesus at the beginning of Jesus' ministry (Matthew 4:1-11). Satan dangled before Jesus perverted means to accomplish legitimate ends. Certainly eating when he was hungry, gaining recognition as a spiritual leader, and reigning over the earth were part of Jesus' plan. But Jesus' way was a different way, a less direct method of achieving the same goals. Satan takes legitimate desires and twists them. The desire for sex, for example, can be twisted into pornography or sex outside of marriage. Good desire, wrong fulfillment. The desire to feed one's family can be fulfilled by stealing or by hard work. But work is not the easy way.

The devil plays on our own desires (James 1:14-15) and tries to convince us that shortcuts will get us there better than the right way.

Resisting the devil means to stop flirting with his temptations. To say "no" to him and "yes" to God.

"He will flee from you." Strange, isn't it, what great power a little word from a humble believer can do to the devil. As Martin Luther put it in his great hymn "A Mighty Fortress Is Our God" – "... a little word can fell him."

3. "Come near to God, and he will come near to you" (4:8a)

What is the problem with double-mindedness? So long as we entertain thoughts of sin, and serve them tea in our living room, we relegate God to the porch. When we flirt with sin in our minds, we necessarily break off fellowship with the Father. So resisting the devil (the negative) is followed by drawing near to God (the positive), resolving our double-minded condition.

---

[12] *Anthistēmi*, BAGD 67.

There's a promise in this verse, too. If we will draw near to God, that is, turn our wills to doing his will, then he will draw near to us, empowering us to follow him, and often, giving us a sense of his presence. We don't *always* experience the joy of his presence – even when he is very present. Sometimes our emotions or other conditions block that sensory awareness. St. John of the Cross wrote about "the dark night of the soul," that difficult time that believers sometimes go through where there is no emotional sense of God, only a faithful submission without the sensory feedback.[13]

4. "Wash your hands and purify your hearts" (4:8b)

James commands us sinners, "wash your hands." What does this mean? He tells us to "purify our hearts," but isn't God the only One who can cleanse us? James is well aware of the necessity for God's *grace*; what he's talking about in this exhortation is *our* job.

"Wash your hands, you sinners" recalls the Prophet Isaiah's message from God to his people:

> "Your hands are full of blood;
> wash and make yourselves clean.
> Take your evil deeds out of my sight!
> Stop doing wrong,
> learn to do right...." (Isaiah 1:15-17)

Washing one's hands is another way of saying, "stop doing wrong". We see a similar figure in the Book of Revelation. John sees a multitude in heaven wearing white robes and praising God. One of the Elders tells who this group is: "These are they who have come out of the great tribulation; they have washed their robes and made them white in the blood of the Lamb" (7:14). No, they didn't save themselves. But they "washed" their robes, they turned from their sin, and were cleansed by Christ's sacrifice on their behalf.

"Purify your hearts, you double-minded," is the second part of this directive. We must stop doing wrong (wash our hands), and then turn our wills decisively to God's will (purify our hearts). The double-mindedness must go. We must decide which way to go and turn to it wholeheartedly. No longer is our will divided, but now our will is "integrated" with our faith and love for God, and we gain "integrity" again.

5. "Grieve, mourn, and wail" (4:9)

True sorrow for sin is not being sorry that you were caught, but sorry that your heart was so hard that you could commit this affront to God. So long as sin is just in the moral category of "bad deeds," it can be looked at as an unfortunate phase of our lives. But

---

[13] See Richard J. Foster, *Prayer: Finding the Heart's True Home* (HarperSanFrancisco, 1992), chapter 2.

when sin is looked at as a proud and independent spirit that stands up to God and deliberately goes the opposite way to His, then we see its personal and ugly side. It is not only morally wrong, it is personal rebellion against the One who loves us. It violates a personal trust, a personal allegiance, a spiritual marriage vow. It is about a relationship. Adultery is bad because it is a taboo sexual relationship. But it is devastating because of what it does to the relationship between husband and wife. We are "married" to God, and our flirtations with the world are in defiance of our Husband.

The appropriate response is grief. It is more than acknowledging our sin; it is owning up to our guilt. I know that talking about guilt is not politically correct. But a sense of guilt is the necessary precursor to genuine heart repentance. Old fashioned revival meetings in the 1800s in the US often included a "mourner's bench" where those convicted of their sins would sit as they worked through this grief and came to a place of repentance. It's still good medicine for the sin-sick soul in our own day.

6. "Humble yourselves before the Lord and he will lift you up" (4:10)

James now sums it up. "Humble yourselves!" The word "humble" is Greek *tapeinoō*, which literally means "lower, make low" and figuratively, "humble, make humble" in a good sense.[14] James has been talking in this chapter about roots of pride and an independent spirit within us: selfishness, hedonism, flirting with sin, spiritual pride that thinks we know better than God what's good for us. The antidote is to recognize our rebellions as foolishness, acknowledge them ("confession"), turn from them ("repentance"), and come before God again as his humble servants rather than his independent-minded subjects. "Humble yourselves!" is a command. It requires submission to God – and an ongoing humility in contrast to a life lived in rebellion against God.

The second half of this command is a promise: "He will lift you up." God doesn't want a bunch of groveling, servile disciples, but those who can stand before him with joy. He wants and promises to lift us up out of our guilt and misery to a place of wholeness and right standing ("righteousness"). Healthy Christianity isn't guilt-ridden, but joy-filled!

Q3. (4:6-10) Verses 7-10 contain 10 different commands. Why are these actions so vital? In what way do they go against our nature? Which of these commands is most difficult for you?

http://www.joyfulheart.com/forums/index.php?act=ST&f=64&t=293

---

[14] *Tapeinoō*, BAGD 804-805.

Critics and Pickers (4:11-12)

The next several verses give examples of presumption, behavior habits that are anything but humble.

> "[11] Brothers, do not slander one another. Anyone who speaks against his brother or judges him speaks against the law and judges it. When you judge the law, you are not keeping it, but sitting in judgment on it. [12] There is only one Lawgiver and Judge, the one who is able to save and destroy. But you–who are you to judge your neighbor?" (4:11-12)

"Brothers, do not slander one another," says James. Why does he bring up slander? Because people in his church were slandering each other. Of course, they wouldn't want to call it slander. Perhaps "creative criticism." The Greek word is *katalaleō*, "speak against, speak evil of, defame, slander."[15] William Tyndale's early translation of the New Testament uses the word "backbite."

If you've been around church much then you've one person speaking against another. Probably you've done it, too. Some people, of course, are fair game. You can say horrible things about a president and his wife and call it political speech. People constantly take shots at a pastor they don't like as well as the last one. They criticize the spouse and children, too, when they don't exhibit the requisite perfection. You expect that of unbelievers, but when Christians – family members – do this, it hurts terribly.

What's wrong with speaking against someone? It is wrong because it conflicts strongly with the law of love. The Apostle Paul reminds us,

> "Love is patient, love is kind. It does not envy, it does not boast, it is not proud. It is not rude, it is not self-seeking, it is not easily angered, it keeps no record of wrongs. Love does not delight in evil but rejoices with the truth. It always protects, always trusts, always hopes, always perseveres. Love never fails." (1 Corinthians 13:4-8).

Certainly "love" requires us to speak truth, even when it is difficult to do so. But we are required to speak the truth lovingly (Ephesians 4:15). Would we speak against the person in their presence? Is our speech loving? Is it fair? Is it kind? Does it come from offended pride?

James says "Anyone who speaks against his brother or judges him speaks against the law and judges it. When you judge the law, you are not keeping it, but sitting in judgment on it" (4:11-12). How is speaking against a brother like speaking against the law? When a Christian speaks against someone, he is setting himself up as a judge – but

---

[15] *Katalaleō*, BAGD 412.

a judge who is prejudiced, lacking all the facts, and failing to hear the accused speak in his own defense. The evil speaker sets himself against two of God's laws:

> "Do not go about spreading slander among your people" (Leviticus 19:16) *and*
> The Royal Law: "Love your neighbor as yourself" (James 2:8)

The evil speaker takes upon himself the role of deciding which laws to apply to himself, and which to the accused. "There is only one Lawgiver and Judge," James says. "But who are you to judge your neighbor" (4:12).[16]

Q4. (4:11-12) In what way does bad-mouthing a neighbor cause you to be a judge of the law? Why is it tempting to bad-mouth others, do you think?

http://www.joyfulheart.com/forums/index.php?act=ST&f=64&t=294

Prayer

Father, forgive the selfishness that is at the root of so many of my sins, and please help me to replace selfishness with humility and voluntary submission to you. Thank you for your grace and patience. Help me not to presume upon them. In Jesus' name, I pray. Amen.

Key Verses

> "When you ask, you do not receive, because you ask with wrong motives, that you may spend what you get on your pleasures." (James 4:3)

> "You adulterous people, don't you know that friendship with the world is hatred toward God? Anyone who chooses to be a friend of the world becomes an enemy of God." (James 4:4)

> "But he gives us more grace. That is why Scripture says:
>   'God opposes the proud
>   but gives grace to the humble.'
> Submit yourselves, then, to God. Resist the devil, and he will flee from you." (James 4:6-7)

> "Humble yourselves before the Lord, and he will lift you up." (James 4:10)

---

[16] For more on slander, see my article "Coming to Grips with Gossip," (www.joyfulheart.com/maturity/gossip.htm).

7. Learning Patience in an Instant Age (4:13-5:12)

These verses speak directly to the impatience and self-indulgence of today's middle class. We want our way and we want it now! We will determine our future course and make it happen! We insist on having our way as much as any rich person of the first century. In fact, we are richer than the wealthy class in James' day. James' exhortation isn't just for *them*, but for *us* too.

This passage examines:

1. The presumption of self-determination (4:13-16)
2. Sins of omission (4:17)
3. The moral bankruptcy of those who oppress the poor (5:1-6)
4. The patience necessary to endure the Lord's coming (5:7-11)
5. The important simplicity of "yes" and "no" (5:12)

The Lord Willing (4:13-16)

We are presumptuous when we speak against our Christian brothers and sisters. We're also presumptuous when we flatly state what we're going to do in days to come, as if we could control the future.

> "Now listen, you who say, 'Today or tomorrow we will go to this or that city, spend a year there, carry on business and make money.' Why, you do not even know what will happen tomorrow. What is your life? You are a mist that appears for a little while and then vanishes. Instead, you ought to say, 'If it is the Lord's will, we will live and do this or that.' As it is, you boast and brag. All such boasting is evil." (4:13-16)

Humility is the antithesis of boasting. We need to train ourselves to speak with this kind of humility when we project actions into the future. "The Lord willing, I plan to get a degree in law and become an attorney," shows a reliance on God. "With God's help, I hope to build the largest construction company in Colusa County," may be ambitious, but it shows reliance on God, also. Humility is the key idea here.

I've heard people use the phrase, "The Lord willing", however, as a kind of spiritual "cop-out."

> "Bill, can we count on you to be here next Saturday to help us repair the roof?"

> "Oh, the Lord willing."

Do you think Bill will *really* come? We aren't to shroud lack of commitment with spiritual jargon. Let your "Yes" be yes, and your "No," no (5:12). Humility about the future is what God desires in us, not fuzziness.

Impatience with the Lord's Will

James' discussion of having patience really begins in the previous section where he admonishes us, "Submit yourselves, then, to God" (4:7). When we submit to God, we become willing to wait for God, rather than to try to produce instant results by our own actions.

Verses 13-16 skewer those who say such things as, "Today or tomorrow we will go to this or that city, spend a year there, carry on business and make money" (4:13). Who talks like that? The poor can't afford to travel on a whim, they are tied to their jobs – and in the first century, to subsistence farming – and aren't entrepreneurs. The rich are often arrogant enough to act as if they are master of their futures and their fortunes.

James' words remind me of Jesus' parable of the Rich Fool. The same arrogance and presumption are there:

> "The ground of a certain rich man produced a good crop. He thought to himself, 'What shall I do? I have no place to store my crops.'
> "Then he said, 'This is what I'll do. I will tear down my barns and build bigger ones, and there I will store all my grain and my goods. And I'll say to myself, "You have plenty of good things laid up for many years. Take life easy; eat, drink and be merry."'
> "But God said to him, 'You fool! This very night your life will be demanded from you. Then who will get what you have prepared for yourself?'
> "This is how it will be with anyone who stores up things for himself but is not rich toward God." (Luke 12:16-21)

You and I can be just as impatient, however. We sometimes have the means to make bold plans for the future. Do we seek the Lord before making decisions? Do we wait on the Lord or just plunge headlong? God keep us from the arrogance of the rich fool!

Q1. (4:13-16) What danger is James warning us about in verses 13-16? How can we be humble in our planning without being indecisive and wishy-washy?
http://www.joyfulheart.com/forums/index.php?act=ST&f=64&t=295

The Good We Ought to Do (4:17)

"Anyone, then, who knows the good he ought to do and doesn't do it, sins." (4:17)

The final sentence of chapter 4 sums up James' emphasis on presumption and humility. He has reminded the readers of their duty to "walk humbly with their God." This is a divine requirement (Micah 6:8). To know of this requirement but ignore it in everyday life constitutes sin in and of itself.

But this concept in a wider context provides an important understanding of sin. The only specific definition of sin in the New Testament is 1 John 3:4: "Sin is lawlessness" (NIV) or "Sin is the transgression of the law" (KJV). This definition focuses negatively on failure to observe the clear statement of the law.

But James introduces another definition: "Anyone, then, who knows the good he ought to do and doesn't do it, sins" (4:17). This is the sin of omission, quite in keeping with much of Jesus' teaching about the failure to do right. Consider:

- The Parable of the Good Samaritan (Luke 10:30-37), where the priest and Levite are condemned for their failure to help their wounded Jewish brother.
- The Parable of the Talents (Matthew 18:23-35), where one servant is condemned for inaction.
- The Parable of the Rich Man and Lazarus (Luke 16:19-31), where the rich man is condemned for failing to share his wealth with the poor man.
- The Parable of the Sheep and the Goats (Matthew 25:31-46), where the "goats" are condemned and the "sheep" approved for the way they help the poor, thirsty, naked, and imprisoned.

In each of these, sins of omission are condemned while acts of positive right are applauded. Christianity does not consist in avoiding wrong – a kind of negativism towards evil– but in doing right. Christianity is about loving our neighbor with random acts of righteousness. We're not to live our lives in mortal fear of sinning and thus compulsively doing good in order to save ourselves from hell. That motive isn't healthy or loving, but essentially selfish.

This Royal Law of Love is much harder to define than the letter of the written law – it is creative and freeing and positive. It is the law that liberates us. The Royal Law allows the Holy Spirit to lead us into the next hours and days with joy and expectation. This kind of living is what God designed us for. To fall short of this is to miss the essence of the Christian message. To fall short of this is tragic. To fall short of this is sin.

Impatience of the Wealthy (5:1-6)

> "[1] Now listen, you rich people, weep and wail because of the misery that is coming upon you. [2] Your wealth has rotted, and moths have eaten your clothes. [3] Your gold and silver are corroded. Their corrosion will testify against you and eat your flesh like fire. You have hoarded wealth in the last days. [4] Look! The wages you failed to pay the workmen who mowed your fields are crying out against you. The cries of the harvesters have reached the ears of the Lord Almighty. [5] You have lived on earth in luxury and self-indulgence. You have fattened yourselves in the day of slaughter. [6] You have condemned and murdered innocent men, who were not opposing you." (5:1-6)

In these verses James indicts the rich. Though they see themselves as rich, he warns that the Day soon approaches that will exhibit what has become of their precious things:

- Wealth has rotted
- Fine clothes have become moth-eaten
- Gold and silver have corroded

But is wealth itself evil? No. A number of God's choice servants have been wealthy, such as Abraham, David, Solomon, Job, Joseph of Arimathea, Barnabas, Lydia, and others. It is not wealth, per se, but how one gains and uses one's wealth that can lead to sin. James indicts the rich with these sins:

Hoarding wealth and not sharing it The word translated "hoarded wealth" (NIV) or "heaped treasure together" (KJV) is Greek *thesaurizō*, "store up, gather, save."[1] Saving for the future is prudent, but this isn't what James has in mind. James' brother, the Lord Jesus, had preached on this theme:

> "Do not store up for yourselves treasures on earth, where moth and rust destroy, and where thieves break in and steal. But store up for yourselves treasures in heaven, where moth and rust do not destroy, and where thieves do not break in and steal. For where your treasure is, there your heart will be also." (Matthew 6:19-21)

According to Judaism of Jesus' day, one stored up treasures in heaven by giving alms to the poor (Mark 10:21). To hoard one's wealth without assisting the poor is a symptom of greed – greed that has captured one's heart. The rich can be guilty of the sin of greed.

Withholding just compensation from one's employees. Those of us who are employers have a special responsibility before God to pay our employees adequately and promptly. And I suppose it extends to paying those promptly from whom we receive goods and services – paying our bills. We cannot, must not defraud those who have a financial claim on us. The rich in James' day did this all too often.

---

[1] *Thesaurizō*, BAGD 361.

Living in luxury (softness) and self-indulgence. What luxuries were enjoyed by the rich in the First Century? Servants, indoor plumbing (at least by some of the Romans), special imported foods and beverages, fine clothes, ready transportation. Now consider some of the things *you* consider necessities that your parents considered luxuries. We enjoy many luxuries.

Are luxuries bad or wrong? The word translated "live in luxury" in 5:5 is Greek *tryphaō*, "to lead a life of luxury or self-indulgence, revel, carouse,"[2] from *tryptō*, "to break down, to enervate, thus, to lead a soft life."[3] The luxuries that wealth can afford are not bad. A few decades ago outhouses were the norm in many areas. There's no virtue in foreswearing porcelain toilets. It's the "soft life" that James is getting at. The ideas is further conveyed by the word NIV translates "self-indulgence," Greek *spatalaō*, "live luxuriously or voluptuously, in indulgence."[4]

When we pamper ourselves and indulge our every whim we become arrogant. We can come to expect this standard of living as our right. We can easily begin to make decisions based on our own creature comfort rather than on God's will. Let me give you an example. In the US a generation ago, Sunday night services were the norm in many denominations. In nearly every denomination, they have given way to Sunday evening television. It's too much trouble to hitch up 175 horsepower to the old car in order to drive in 10 minutes to the church. Our luxuries can easily capture our will unless we resist the tempter.

Condemning and killing the innocent. To those for whom their standard of living is all-important, human life itself can become less valuable. Twin evils related to the cheapness of human life are prominent in our high tech world: abortion and euthanasia. I doubt that this is what James had in mind. He was thinking of how the rich snuff out their opposers, but I can't help but wonder....

Q2. (5:5-6) What is the spiritual danger of our demand for comfort and luxury? *Extra credit:* **How might our demand for low-priced goods and services cause us to (1) oppress our own employees or (2) cause workers in this country or abroad to be under paid or oppressed? How does all this relate to the need for patience?**
http://www.joyfulheart.com/forums/index.php?act=ST&f=64&t=296

---

[2] *Tryphaō*, BAGD 828.
[3] Robertson, *Word Pictures*.
[4] *Spatalaō*, BAGD 761.

The Coming of the Lord (5:7-8)

"⁷Be patient, then, brothers, until the Lord's coming. See how the farmer waits for the land to yield its valuable crop and how patient he is for the autumn and spring rains. ⁸You too, be patient and stand firm, because the Lord's coming is near. ⁹Don't grumble against each other, brothers, or you will be judged. The Judge is standing at the door!" (5:7-8)

In contrast to a mindset that thinks of fulfilling every want and desire right now, we have the mindset of the humble Christian believer. James speaks about the Second Coming of Christ twice in as many verses:

"Be patient, then, brothers, until the Lord's coming...." (5:7)

"You too, be patient and stand firm, because the Lord's coming is near." (5:8)

Throughout the New Testament we see the clear promise of Christ's return at the end of the age. I've compiled a number of these scriptures in an appendix so you can see their scope. Jesus told parables of a man who goes away on a long trip and puts his servants in charge. Then he returns quickly to find them either drunk and abusive or faithful and eager, and rewards them. Jesus gives us signs to expect – wars and rumors of wars, earthquakes, the appearance of the Antichrist. Some Christian teachers have imagined that we can predict the Day of his return. But the purpose of the scriptures is to help us to be ready, not to know of a certainty when our Master will return.

Biblical Christians live in two worlds, the here and now where we work and love and have babies and witness for Christ, and in heavenly places, in an intimate relationship to God who promises to wrap up events on this earth in righteousness and justice. We live in the Now but with a constant expectation of the Day to come.

We live, not just for the here and now, but for the Day when the world will change, when Christ will be revealed, when justice will reign, where every private action will become public and nothing will be hidden. Theologians call this an eschatological perspective, and the study of the end times is called eschatology. It comes from two Greek words, *eschatos*, "the end" and *logos*, "thing, word."

Sometimes we get impatient or unbelieving. When I was a young man I expected Christ to return within a year or two. Events in the Middle East seemed to foreshadow his coming. Then it didn't happen. Perhaps within my lifetime, I thought. But it is vital that I retain this expectation and not get jaded. Peter speaks to this question.

"In the last days scoffers will come, scoffing and following their own evil desires. They will say, 'Where is this "coming" he promised?' ...

But do not forget this one thing, dear friends: With the Lord a day is like a thousand years, and a thousand years are like a day. The Lord is not slow in keeping his promise, as some understand slowness. He is patient with you, not wanting anyone to perish, but everyone to come to repentance. But the day of the Lord will come like a thief...." (2 Peter 3:3-4, 8-10)

That's how Christ taught us to understand it. Be ready, he said. Stay awake and alert. The Son of Man will come at a time you do not expect. Be ready.

Are you ready? Am I? James echoes Jesus' words: "Be patient, then, brothers, until the Lord's coming" (5:7).

Patience and Endurance

The verb in 5:7, 8 translated "be patient" is Greek *makrothymeō*, a compound word, formed from *makros*, "long, lasting long," and *thymos*, "that which is moved and which moves, vital force," similar in meaning to the word *pneuma*, "spirit."[5] So a literal translation of *makrothymeō* might be "to be of a long spirit, not to lose heart."[6] In verse 10 we also see the noun form, *makrothymia*, "patience." Having the long-term view in an instant culture is not always easy, but God calls us to it.

Another word used in 5:13 is Greek *hypomenō*, another compound word, from *hupo* – under and *menō* – to remain, abide. *Hypomenō* means "remain instead of fleeing, stand one's ground, hold out, endure' in trouble, affliction, persecution."[7] Both the verb and the noun occur in verse 11, and are translated "persevered/perseverance" (NIV), "steadfast/steadfastness" (RSV), "endured/endurance" (NASB), and "endure/patience" (KJV). Part of faithfulness is standing our ground and not moving off of it. Perhaps the classic statement of this is in Ephesians 6:13:

"Therefore put on the full armor of God, so that when the day of evil comes, you may be able to stand your ground, and after you have done everything, to stand."

In battle, victory is not always moving forward to take the next hill, it often means to remain still standing at the end of the battle after your position has been attacked by the enemy. Endurance is surely a fruit of the Spirit's work in our lives.

James uses a similar phrase in verse 8: to "establish your hearts" (RSV, KJV) or "stand firm" (NIV). The verb is Greek *sterizō*, which means, "set up, fix (firmly), establish, support," figuratively, "confirm, establish, strengthen."[8] There comes a time to make up

---

[5] Friedrich Büchsel, *thymos, ktl.*, TDNT 3:167.

[6] *Makrothymeō*, Thayer 387.

[7] *Hypomenō*, BAGD 845-846.

[8] *Sterizō*, BAGD 768.

our mind that, God helping us, we shall not be moved by the things happening around us, like the old spiritual says:

> "I shall not be, I shall not be moved,
> I shall not be, I shall not be moved,
> Just like a tree planted by the water, Lord,
> I shall not be moved."

Patience for the Early and Latter Rains (5:7)

> "Be patient, then, brothers, until the Lord's coming. See how the farmer waits for the land to yield its valuable crop and how patient he is for the autumn and spring rains." (5:7)

James uses the farmer as an example. First Century people were much closer to agriculture than our society today. While 70% of the US population, for example, is clustered in urban areas and agriculture employs only 6% of the population, in Jesus' day it was very much different. Nearly everyone lived in villages and went out to work their land. They knew about the vicissitudes of the weather. In Palestine there were two rainy seasons: the autumn rains (the "early rains") and the spring rains ("the latter rains"). Both had to fall for the crops to ripen and be ready for harvest. There was no use trying to hurry it up. Farmers learned patience.

But harvest was another thing. There is a prime time to harvest a particular crop. It varies, of course, from crop to crop. Harvest time is affected by temperature, sunlight, rain or irrigation, insects, and even impending weather conditions. When it is time to harvest, farmers sometimes work day and night to get in the crop, because if they do not harvest at the right time, they can lose the entire crop or greatly reduce its value.

Jesus' Second Coming can be compared to a harvest. There's no hurrying up the time. We must be patient, and hopeful, sure of eventual harvest. But like the farmer, we must be ready. When the harvest is here there is no time for waiting. It must happen today.

Q3. (5:7-8) What can happen to us Christians if we lack the patience to eagerly expect Christ's return? Why is patience so vital?

http://www.joyfulheart.com/forums/index.php?act=ST&f=64&t=297

Patience vs. Grumbling (5:9)

> "Don't grumble against each other, brothers, or you will be judged. The Judge is standing at the door!" (5:9)

Complaining can be so sweet sometimes. Just griping gives you a chance to get some of that internal frustration out where others can feel sorry for you. James had a word for it: grumbling. The Greek word is *stenazō*, "sigh, groan" because of an undesirable circumstance. With the preposition *kata* is has the meaning "groan against, complain of someone."[9]

But our sighs and groans signal impatience and discontent. Why is God so hard on complainers? Because our grumbling about people is a thinly veiled way of complaining about God.

The Israelites had been enslaved in Egypt for hundreds of years. Then God sent an deliverer, Moses, who wasn't any too happy himself to be in that role. But he went. No sooner than he began to obey God, however, people began to complain. He went to Pharaoh with God's message and came away with no more than the command that the Hebrews had to find their own straw to make bricks (Exodus 5). The people blamed him. Once the people were free – and hemmed in by the Red Sea – they complained again (Exodus 14). Each time the Lord brought them through one victory they rejoiced. But as soon as another problem came they grumbled again. They complained about lack of food; God sent manna. They complained about lack of meat; God sent quail. (Exodus 16). They complained about thirst; God brought water out of the rock (Exodus 17). It went on that way for 40 years. Problem, grumble. Problem, complain. Paul wrote of this generation of Israelites:

> "Now these things occurred as examples to keep us from setting our hearts on evil things as they did.... And do not grumble, as some of them did–and were killed by the destroying angel" (1 Corinthians 10:6, 10)

> "Do everything without complaining or arguing, so that you may become blameless and pure, children of God without fault in a crooked and depraved generation, in which you shine like stars in the universe" (Philippians 2:14-16).

Moses said with great insight, "You are not grumbling against us, but against the Lord" (Exodus 16:8). God reminded Samuel of a similar lesson: "It is not you they have rejected, but they have rejected me as their king" (1 Samuel 8:7). Either we will be patient or we will be judged by the Judge himself.

---

[9] *Stenazō*, BAGD 766.

There is a very thin line between grumbling and unbelief. Very thin. What are you complaining about? Your children? Your spouse? Your job? Your health? Aren't you perhaps coming dangerously close to blaming God for allowing this situation? God calls you to pray, and then to patiently trust him to work out your problems. Patiently, with l-o-n-g-suffering.

If you grumble at the least provocation, where's your faith in God? Faith without actions is dead faith, James has reminded us. Real faith requires patience. The patience of Job.

Q4. (5:9) What does our grumbling and complaining say about us? About our faith? About our patience?
http://www.joyfulheart.com/forums/index.php?act=ST&f=64&t=298

Patience of the Prophets and Job (5:10-11)

"¹⁰ Brothers, as an example of patience in the face of suffering, take the prophets who spoke in the name of the Lord. ¹¹ As you know, we consider blessed those who have persevered. You have heard of Job's perseverance and have seen what the Lord finally brought about. The Lord is full of compassion and mercy." (5:10-11)

We Christians are not only called to exercise patience when we are tired of waiting, but we are to be steadfast in the face of suffering (*kakopatheia*, verse 11).

Patient suffering isn't very popular in the ME-generation, but that's what God sometimes calls us to. James gives us two examples of patient suffering.

The prophets spoke God's word even when it wasn't popular to do so. Jeremiah, the "weeping prophet" was imprisoned, called a traitor, and rejected by the very people God sent him to help. Many prophets have been killed for their courage. John the Baptist is an example of a New Testament prophet who was imprisoned for speaking God's word and then beheaded on a whim.

The other example James gives us is Job. Here was a righteous, God-fearing man who had everything. Then, for reasons he was never told, lost everything – wealth, children, health. His wife told him to curse God and die, but he refused.

"He replied, 'You are talking like a foolish woman. Shall we accept good from God, and not trouble?' In all this, Job did not sin in what he said." (Job 2:10)

His "friends" came to comfort him, but ended up accusing him of sin, and becoming belligerent if he didn't confess. Instead, he looked to God to vindicate him – in this life or in the next.

> "I know that my Redeemer lives,
> and that in the end he will stand upon the earth.
> And after my skin has been destroyed,
> yet in my flesh I will see God...." (Job 19:25-26)

He persevered. And though God never told him why these things had taken place, God blessed him during his lifetime, and restored to Job more than he had lost.

James concludes his allusion to Job's life: "The Lord is full of compassion and mercy" (5:11b). The word translated "full of compassion" is Greek *polysplanchnos*, "sympathetic, compassionate, merciful,"[10] a compound word from *poly*, "much, great" and *splanchnon*, "bowels, intestines," regarded as the seat of tender affections, especially kindness, benevolence, compassion.[11] If you've ever felt your stomach tied up in knots, it is because of the close relationship to emotions, the nervous system, and this part of your body. The word translated "mercy" is Greek *oiktirmōn*, "merciful, compassionate."[12] No matter what you may be going through, God never stops loving you.

You may never know why you have to undergo the hardships you do. God knows, you don't. But if you can live your life in praise rather than petulance, in confession rather than complaint, you – like Job – can shine as God's trophy in the face of all Satan's cynical sneers. Why must you develop patience? So you can glorify God.

Patience with Our Words (5:12)

> "Above all, my brothers, do not swear–not by heaven or by earth or by anything else.
> Let your "Yes" be yes, and your "No," no, or you will be condemned." (5:12)

The final verse in our section, about making rash oaths, may seem out of context, but it's not. We aren't so given to this as people of a former generation. But in their impatience people used to make sacred promises that they would do so-and-so if God did such-and-such. They would "swear," Greek *omnyō*, "to swear; to affirm, promise, threaten, with an oath."[13] This does not mean "to use profane or obscene language" like our English word "swear," but in the sense of "to invoke the name of God in an oath."[14]

---

[10] *Polysplanchnos*, BAGD 689.
[11] *Splanchnon*, Thayer 584.
[12] *Oiktirmōn*, BAGD 561.
[13] *Omnyō*, Thayer 444, BAGD 565-566.
[14] *Merriam Webster's Collegiate Dictionary* (10th edition), p. 1190.

Sometimes in our impatience and frustration we say stupid things and make stupid promises. But this doesn't please God. James' older brother Jesus spoke about this problem, too:

> "Again, you have heard that it was said to the people long ago, 'Do not break your oath, but keep the oaths you have made to the Lord.' But I tell you, Do not swear at all: either by heaven, for it is God's throne; or by the earth, for it is his footstool; or by Jerusalem, for it is the city of the Great King. And do not swear by your head, for you cannot make even one hair white or black. Simply let your 'Yes' be 'Yes,' and your 'No,' 'No'; anything beyond this comes from the evil one." (Matthew 5:33-37)

Let your "Yes" mean yes. Not confused with rash promises and complications. Just yes. Or no. A life of patience comes to be a life of simplicity. Trusting God rather than trying to manipulate people and situations with our grand-sounding promises.

Be Patient

"Be patient, then, brothers, until the Lord's coming," James tells us. "Be patient and stand firm.... Don't grumble against each other.... As an example of patience in the face of suffering, take the prophets ... and Job."

"As you know, we consider blessed those who have persevered," says James (5:11a). Is that you? my friend. Are you willing to persevere? Are you willing to sign up for this Christian walk for the long haul? Yes, like the fruit of the earth, they need the early rains, and the latter rains, but eventually the harvest will come, and you will see him in his glory on that Day. Have patience, my friend.

Prayer

Lord, work patience within us. Slow us down to your pace. Help us be willing to wait on you and trust you, even when it hurts to do so. Grant us patience, Lord, because patience is part of your character. In Jesus' name we pray. Amen.

Key Verses

"Anyone, then, who knows the good he ought to do and doesn't do it, sins." (James 4:17)

"Be patient, then, brothers, until the Lord's coming." (James 5:7a)

"Above all, my brothers, do not swear – not by heaven or by earth or by anything else. Let your 'Yes' be yes, and your 'No,' no, or you will be condemned." (James 5:12b)

8. Praying the Prayer of Faith (5:13-20)

Over the course of this brief letter, James has discussed key themes to help Christians mature in the faith:

- Standing firm during trials and temptations,
- Living out the Christian faith in practical ways rather than just studying or hearing it,
- Loving selflessly,
- Taming the tongue,
- Humbling oneself before God,
- Trusting in God rather than in wealth, and
- Exercising patience.

He concludes these traits of a disciple with a call to praying with faith.

Each circumstance of life is a time to pray: trouble, happiness, and sickness – all are an occasion for prayer and worship (5:13). James spends most of his time, however, discussing prayer in time of physical infirmity. How does one pray then, when it is difficult to pray for oneself?

Faith to Ask for Prayer (5:13-14)

"¹³ Is any one of you in trouble? He should pray. Is anyone happy? Let him sing songs of praise. ¹⁴ Is any one of you sick? He should call the elders of the church to pray over him and anoint him with oil in the name of the Lord." (5:13-14)

James instructs the sick person to "call the elders of the church...." I think it's significant that James doesn't put the burden of prayer on the sick person; his responsibility is to call for others to pray, not just to pray alone. Of course, the sick person will ask God to help him – that's taken for granted. We are always to pray, about everything. But when illness becomes serious, the sick person doesn't need to rely only upon his own faith; he is to call for the elders. (Of course, this isn't to be a new "law," but a principle that helps us recognize faith.)

As I've studied the gospels, I'm impressed by the way in which Jesus generally ministers. Some faith is a necessary environment for healing to occur. When Jesus ministered in his hometown of Nazareth, the Scripture says, "He *could not* do any miracles there ... and he was amazed at their lack of faith" (Mark 6:5-6). Jesus generally doesn't go out looking for sick people, they come to him for healing – their coming is a sign of faith, or at least of curiosity. And when they come, Jesus sometimes asks a question to determine their faith or to motivate their faith. In two instances, blind men called out to Jesus. He asked them:

> "Do you believe that I am able to do this?" (Matthew 9:28)
> "What do you want me to do for you?" (Matthew 20:32)

This is not a just a test of faith, but an encouragement to faith, a stimulus to believe. Jairus comes asking Jesus to heal his daughter, but when messengers come from home to report her death, Jesus can see Jairus faltering. "Don't be afraid; just believe," Jesus assures him, "and she will be healed" (Luke 8:50).

To the epileptic boy's father who asked if Jesus could do anything, Jesus replied, "If *you* can. Everything is possible for him who believes." Immediately the boy's father exclaimed, "I do believe; help me overcome my unbelief!" (Mark 9:23) But it wasn't only the father's faith involved in healing. Why had the disciples failed to cast out the demon causing the illness? Jesus explained it, "because you have so little faith" (Matthew 17:20). Whose faith was most vital to healing? The father's or the disciples'? I think the *disciples'* faith was more crucial. They had much more experience with healing and faith and prayer than the father.

Too often those with healing gifts blame lack of healing on the sick person, rather than take responsibility for our own lack of faith. Yes, "according to your faith will it be done to you" is a principle (as in Matthew 9:29), but it was Jesus' act of faith that accomplished the healing. The sick person (or his father) needs to be open to healing, but the main expectation for faith is upon the One or ones doing the praying, and so it is in James.

In James, the sick person is to "call for the elders of the church," but it is the elders who are responsible to pray the "prayer of faith."

Q1. (5:13-14) According to verse 14, who is to initiate prayer for healing? Why might this be important?
http://www.joyfulheart.com/forums/index.php?act=ST&f=64&t=299

Elders of the Church (5:14)

> "Is any one of you sick? He should call **the elders of the church** to pray over him and anoint him with oil in the name of the Lord" (5:14)

But who are the "elders of the church"? The word "elders" in 5:14 is Greek *presbyteros*, which could designate "an old man" or an official, "elder."[1] Are the elders in James' Letter church officials, or mature believers? I would guess that James is referring to the elders as the mature leaders in a congregation who "rule" (Titus 1:5; 1 Timothy 5:17). In James' day, these leaders were looked to because of their faith.

In our day, sadly, we have elders who are leaders characterized not so much by faith, but by longevity and political influence. Some of these are the last people I'd want to pray for me. How many times have I heard older men pray for the sick in such a halting, over-qualified way: "Lord, if it be in your will to heal this person, do it, but if not, give us the ability to accept suffering and death which is our lot." You know this kind of prayer. You don't find this sort of healing prayer in the Bible! In the Bible, people expected God to heal, rather than expected him not to. You find bold prayers, not prayers laden with phrasing to protect us from responsibility in the likelihood that God doesn't heal. We aren't to pray like lawyers!

How can we regain bold faith? By immersing ourselves in the Word, and ministering alongside those who *do* have faith for healing.

The late John Wimber, founder of the Vineyard Fellowship movement, had a powerful influence on my life. During the 1980s he taught MC501 at Fuller Theological Seminary with Dr. Peter Wagner, a course entitled "Signs, Wonders, and Church Growth." It was probably the most popular course on campus until it was finally shut down by the powers that be, who seemed to act as if seminaries were designed for academic learning of ministry, rather than practical learning of faith. (That statement, of course, isn't entirely fair, but that's the way it seemed at the time.)[2]

On class nights I would sit and watch as Wimber would pray for those who desired healing prayer. It was tremendously instructive because Wimber used it as a laboratory in which to teach. Microphone on so he could be heard by the hundreds who the packed the hall, Wimber would interview the candidate for healing, share with the class what the Lord was showing him about the person and about how to pray, and speak the actual prayer. I'd had enough personal experience with prayer for the sick to know that what I was seeing was real, not some fakery.

---

[1] *Presbyteros*, BAGD 700.
[2] See John Wimber and Kevin N. Springer, *Power Healing* (HarperSanFrancisco, reprint 1991).

One of the most poignant moments was when Wimber shared the experience of when he and his team went to England to pray for David Watson, a prominent evangelical Anglican priest and evangelist, who was suffering from cancer. Though Wimber's team had prayed for many people and seen many miracles, when they prayed for Watson, they did not see the healing, and Wimber's dear friend David Watson gradually succumbed to his illness. You could hear the sorrow and bewilderment in Wimber's voice as he shared this with the class. It was much like healer-evangelist Katherine Kuhlman's response to her *Christianity Today* interviewer in the late 1960s, who asked her about those who weren't healed. "I don't understand it," she replied, "but I weep much over it."

No, not everyone we pray for will be healed. But that shouldn't keep us from praying with faith. Even those whom Jesus healed eventually died.

Maturity in Christian leaders isn't flabby faith that never asks for miracles. Rather it is tried and true faith that knows the Lord, and isn't afraid to ask the God of the Impossible to do the impossible. May our present-day elders reclaim this maturity of faith! My point is that we are to call for the elders, not because they have an official position, but because they are mature believers who are full of faith, and (hopefully) are best equipped in the congregation to pray "the prayer of faith."

Q2. (5:14) What is the elders' role in prayer for the sick? What must be their spiritual qualifications for this ministry of prayer?
http://www.joyfulheart.com/forums/index.php?act=ST&f=64&t=300

Anointing with Oil (5:14)

> "Is any one of you sick? He should call the elders of the church to pray over him and **anoint him with oil** in the name of the Lord" (5:14)

The elders are instructed to "prayer over [the sick person] and anoint him with oil in the name of the Lord" (5:14). I've read arguments that the oil was used for its believed medicinal properties, much like the Good Samaritan who treated the wounded man on the road from Jerusalem to Jericho by "pouring on oil and wine" (Luke 10:34).[3] But while I don't doubt that people of the time used oil for its medicinal properties, I don't think this is what James has in mind in our passage.

There are four reasons I believe this anointing with oil was a sacred act of faith:

---

[3] Adamson (*James*, pp. 197-198) takes this tack.

1. Elders are administering the anointing, rather than just anyone,

2. Prayer accompanies the anointing; bold, powerful, believing prayer,

3. The name of the Lord is part of this anointing, and

4. The scripture provides ample precedent for using oil as part of a sacred ritual or act of faith.

It's a little recognized fact that Jesus' disciples "anointed many sick people with oil and healed them" (Mark 6:13). Now why would they do that? No doubt Jesus instructed them to do so, and perhaps occasionally did so himself, though we find no other mention in the gospels.

In the Old Testament, anointing with oil is used to set apart or ordain leaders, priests, and holy things (Exodus 29:4-7; 30:22-25, 31-33; Leviticus 8:10-12; 1 Samuel 9:16; 10:1; 16:3, 12-13, etc.) In a most striking passage, Samuel anoints David to be king instead of Saul:

> "So Samuel took the horn of oil and anointed him in the presence of his brothers, and from that day on the Spirit of the Lord came upon David in power.... Now the Spirit of the Lord had departed from Saul..." (1 Samuel 16:13-14).

In the New Testament, also, the word "anointing" is closely connected with the Holy Spirit:

> "... How God anointed Jesus of Nazareth with the Holy Spirit and power, and how he went around doing good and healing all who were under the power of the devil, because God was with him" (Acts 10:38).

This verse probably refers to the Holy Spirit coming upon Jesus at his baptism (Luke 3:22), empowering his ministry (Luke 4:1, 14), and fulfilling scripture: "the Spirit of the Lord is on me, because he has anointed me to..." (Luke 4:18-19, quoting Isaiah 61:1-2).

Believers, too, have "the anointing you received from him ... as his anointing teaches you about all things, and as that anointing is real, not counterfeit...." (1 John 2:20, 27-28), referring to the promised Holy Spirit (John 14:26; 15:26-27; 16:7, 12-15).

I conclude that anointing with oil was a symbol of the presence of God's powerful Holy Spirit. Was it magical? No, it was symbolic. Oral Roberts, a Pentecostal healing-evangelist active from the 1950s through the 1980s, saw such things as anointing with oil, laying on of hands, etc. as a "point of contact" for a person's faith, a stimulus to faith. I think he's right.

Of course, people can be healed without anointing with oil. Look at Jesus' ministry. People can be healed without the laying on of hands, too. You can find numerous examples in the New Testament. But anointing with oil and the laying on of hands can be a powerful and personal way to minister in the Holy Spirit, and a stimulus to faith.

Should elders always use oil when they pray for the sick, in obedience to this passage in James? No, I don't think this is meant as a restrictive law. But they should be willing to pray, and be open to using whatever God desires to encourage faith and represent the presence of the Lord in the healing moment – and anointing oil can often fit very well indeed.

The Roman Catholic Church uses James 5:14 as the basis for its Sacrament of Extreme Unction ("unction" means anointing), commonly known as "Last Rites." But in the last few decades, movements within the Catholic Church have now recognized that this sacrament should not be reserved just for death, but also performed with the expectation of healing. Certainly, that is what James intended.

In the Name of the Lord (5:14)

> "Is any one of you sick? He should call the elders of the church to pray over him and anoint him with oil **in the name of the Lord**" (5:14)

The next element in James' instruction about healing is to pray and anoint with oil "in the name of the Lord" (5:14). This is referring to the authority we have to invoke God's presence and power and authority by using the name of Jesus. The Greek word is *onoma*, a very common word. Bauer, Arndt, and Gingrich, who studied this word in its various contexts found that the "name" meant "something real, a piece of the very nature of the personality whom it designates, that partakes in his qualities and his powers."[4] We see many examples in the New Testament:

> "I tell you the truth, anyone who has faith in me will do what I have been doing [in context, "works" or "miracles"]. He will do even greater things than these, because I am going to the Father [and at the same time sending to my disciples the Holy Spirit]. And I will do whatever you **ask in my name**, so that the Son may bring glory to the Father. You may **ask me for anything in my name**, and I will do it." (John 14:12-14)

Baptism, too, was to be "in the name of Jesus Christ" (Acts 2:38). Peter and John say to the crippled man seeking alms at the temple gate, "Silver or gold I do not have, but what I have I give you. In the name of Jesus Christ of Nazareth, walk" (Act 3:6). "By faith in the name of Jesus, this man whom you see and know was made strong. It is Jesus' name and the faith that comes through him that has given this complete healing to him, as you can all see" (Acts 3:16).

---

[4] *Onoma*, BAGD 570-573.

James is telling us that to anoint the sick person and pray invoking the name of Jesus is very powerful indeed. This calls the powerful Presence of God Himself into the healing ministry.

Prayer Offered in Faith (5:15)

> "And the prayer offered in faith will make the sick person well; the Lord will raise him up. If he has sinned, he will be forgiven." (5:15)

We've seen several elements in this healing prayer: the faith of the sick person to call for the elders, the presence of mature, faith-filled Christians, their prayers, anointing with oil, and the name of the Lord. But it is faith that James lifts up as the point here. When all is said and done, neither elders, nor oil, nor prayer, nor the name of Jesus effect healing. Rather "the prayer offered in faith" (NIV) or "the prayer of faith" (RSV, KJV). Faith in action is the theme of the Letter of James, and he continues this theme to the end of the letter. Notice that it is the faith of the "pray-er" rather than the "pray-ee" who offers the "effective" (KJV) prayer. Yes, the faith of the sick person is important in asking for prayer, but the elders' "prayer of faith" is what effects the healing.

The "prayer of faith" is said to "save" (KJV, RSV) the sick person, or "make the sick person well" (NIV). The word used here is Greek *sōzō*, a common word that means "save, keep from harm, preserve, rescue." It is found in Classical as well as NT Greek in the sense of "save or free from disease or from demonic possession,"[5] and that is the sense used in our passage. We often look at salvation as spiritual only, but the Bible reflects the view that the spiritual and physical sicknesses are intertwined. Certainly, Jesus' ministry was to the whole person – body, soul, and spirit. He did whatever a person needed to become whole again.

Healing and Forgiveness (5:15c-16)

Nowhere in the New Testament is this close relationship between spiritual and physical illness so visible as this passage.

> "[15c] If he has sinned, he will be forgiven. [16] Therefore confess your sins to each other and pray for each other so that you may be healed. The prayer of a righteous man is powerful and effective." (5:15c-16)

It was common when someone was sick to suppose that he had committed some sin that caused the sickness. That's what Job's "friends" supposed. Some time after Jesus healed a paralyzed man at the Pool of Bethesda, he saw him in the temple, and said,

---

[5] *Sōzō*, BAGD 798-799.

"See, you are well again. Stop sinning or something worse may happen to you" (John 5:14). The rich people in the Corinthian church were guilty of the sins of selfishness and partiality when they fed themselves during the Lord's Supper, but didn't provide for their poor brothers and sisters. Paul says,

> "For anyone who eats and drinks without recognizing the body of the Lord eats and drinks judgment on himself. That is why many among you are weak and sick, and a number of you have fallen asleep" (1 Corinthians 11:29-30).

On the other hand, Jesus makes it clear that sickness isn't *necessarily* caused by sin. You seldom see any rebuke during Jesus' healing ministry. And we read this passage: "

> "As he went along, he saw a man blind from birth. His disciples asked him, 'Rabbi, who sinned, this man or his parents, that he was born blind?'
> 'Neither this man nor his parents sinned,' said Jesus, 'but this happened so that the work of God might be displayed in his life.'" (John 9:1-3)

In our passage, however, James cautions us to consider whether sin *is* part of what is causing the sickness, for he says about the sick person,

> "If he has sinned, he will be forgiven. Therefore confess your sins to each other and pray for each other so that you may be healed." (5:15-16)

In other words, the elders are to assist the sick person to be healed both physically *and* spiritually, if that is the need, since these can affect each other profoundly. I've ministered to people who held in so much hatred and unforgiveness that God was unwilling to heal them until they let it go and got right with God and man.

The Power of Confession (5:16)

> "If he has sinned, he will be forgiven. Therefore confess your sins to each other and pray for each other so that you may be healed." (5:15-16)

Why should confession of sins be so controversial? The Roman Catholic Church institutionalized confession into the Sacrament of Penance (including confession and absolution) by the Tenth Century, based on James 5:16; Matthew 16:19; and John 20:23. During the Reformation, the Protestants protested against the power of the Church, and refused to acknowledge Penance as a sacrament. Confession need only be made to God, they would argue, and not to a priest. Luther taught "the priesthood of the believer."

But I think that we Protestants have thrown the baby out with the bathwater. The roots of the Christian movement were in John the Baptist, who made confessing one's sins part of baptism (Matthew 3:6).

As a pastor I know that some people cannot be freed from certain sins until they will confess them to someone they trust. The Twelve Step Movement, developed in large part by evangelical Anglican priest Sam Shoemaker, took these core principles straight out of the Bible:

> Step 4: Made a searching and fearless moral inventory of ourselves.
> Step 5: Admitted to God, to ourselves, and to another human being, the exact nature of our wrongs.
> Step 6: Were entirely ready to have God remove all the defects of character.

In this kind of encounter, by confessing one's sins to a Christian, the person is making himself accountable for his sin. He is piercing the darkness of this secret that has locked him in this sin for a long time. Once this is done, he can finally let go of this sin to God. Refusal to confess a sin can sometimes mean that the person is still nursing and coddling the sin, and secretly enjoying it. The Christian friend can assure the person making a confession of Almighty God's forgiveness based on 1 John 1:9.

Notice that neither an elder nor a priest is the designated confessor, but Christian believers in general. James says, "Therefore confess your sins to each other and pray for each other so that you may be healed. The prayer of a righteous man is powerful and effective" (5:16). After confession comes prayer, and from the prayer of faith comes healing.

Q3. (5:14-16) In the healing prayer, what is the role of oil? What is the role of the prayer of faith? What is the role of faith? What is the role of confession of sins?
http://www.joyfulheart.com/forums/index.php?act=ST&f=64&t=301

Prayer of a Righteous Man (5:16b-18)

> "¹⁶ᵇ The prayer of a righteous man is powerful and effective. ¹⁷ Elijah was a man just like us. He prayed earnestly that it would not rain, and it did not rain on the land for three and a half years. ¹⁸ Again he prayed, and the heavens gave rain, and the earth produced its crops." (5:16b-18)

James has just opened the door for all Christian believers to be involved in this ministry of confession and prayer for healing – both spiritual and physical. It is as if James can feel your reticence, as if you were saying, "I'm not spiritual enough to do that. My prayers aren't anything special." So James draws your attention to the Prophet Elijah who spoke a word that caused a three-year drought, and another word that ended it.

Wow! Powerful! I could never do that. He must be a great man of God.

Elijah *is* a great man of God. He does courageous and powerful exploits for God. But at other times he is weak and paranoid and fearful and self-important. After he has slain the 450 prophets of Baal on Mount Carmel (1 Kings 18), he flees Jezebel's wrath. He runs for his life into the desert and lies down under a broom tree, physically, emotionally, and spiritually spent. "I have had enough, Lord," he says, "Take my life. I am no better than my ancestors" (1 Kings 19).

Does that sound familiar? It gets worse.

He runs some more until he comes to Mount Sinai (Horeb). When he gets there, God asks him, "What are you doing here, Elijah?"

Elijah answers with whining and excuses, the kind you wouldn't accept from your own children:

> "I have been very zealous for the Lord God Almighty. The Israelites have rejected your covenant, broken down your altars, and put your prophets to death with the sword. I am the only one left, and now they are trying to kill me too." (1 Kings 19:10)

I've caught myself whining to God like that. "Lord, I've sacrificed and done this and that, and who appreciates it? No one! Blah, blah, blah." You know the drill. You've probably said it yourself!

God just listens, and then speaks to Elijah in a still small voice, gives him three tasks to do, and says, "By the way, Elijah. There are still 7,000 who haven't worshipped Baal. You're not the only one, after all."

Elijah the great man of God isn't such a great man after all. So why does James mention him? Because we can identify with Elijah's weaknesses.

As James puts it in verse 17, "Elijah was a man just like us" (NIV) or "Elias was a man subject to like passions as we are" (KJV). The Greek word is *homoiopathēs*, from two words *homoios*, "like, similar, resembling" and *paschō*, "to feel, undergo, be affected". This compound word means "of similar feelings, circumstances, experiences 'with the same nature.'"[6]

James' point is this: if God heard Elijah's prayers, as much a failure as he sometimes was, he will hear your prayers, too.

Verse 16c has a wonderful cadence in the KJV: "The effectual fervent prayer of a righteous man availeth much." Other translations are a bit more down to earth: "The prayer of a righteous man is powerful and effective" (NIV) or "The prayer of a righteous man has great power in its effects" (RSV).

---

[6] *Homoiopathēs*, BAGD 566, also found in Acts 14:15.

Our problem is that we don't believe this. We think that God is a respecter of persons. God hears the prayer of Other People, more Perfect People than I. The truth is that God looks for faith, and where he finds it he can do powerful things. He can forgive your sins. He can forget about your weaknesses. He seeks your faith, your bold faith, for when you offer that to Him, he can use you far beyond your own capacity. Don't forget this truth: "The prayer of a righteous man is powerful and effective."

When I was a young man, a powerful and bold speaker, Costa Dier, came to the local congregation where I worshipped, and was welcomed with a flattering introduction in keeping with his legendary reputation in our church's circles. When he stood up, he said: "Don't introduce me as a 'great man of God.' Rather introduce me as a 'man of a great God.'"

Don't measure by your weaknesses how God can use you. Measure only by God's own strength. The Apostle Paul prayed for the Ephesians,

> "having the eyes of your hearts enlightened, that you may know ... what is the **immeasurable greatness of his power in us who believe**, according to the working of his great might which he accomplished in Christ when he raised him from the dead...." (Ephesians 1:18-20. RSV)

Bring Back Wandering Brothers and Sisters (5:19-20)

James closes his letter with an encouragement for Christians to bring back their brothers and sisters who have wandered from the faith. I've heard this passage used as ammunition in the great debate between Calvinists and Arminians.

But that isn't James' point. He is talking about prayer. He wants us to pray earnestly, not only for Christian believers who are sick and confess their sins, but also for those who have wandered from the truth, and are still out there wandering.

> "My brothers, if one of you should wander from the truth and someone should bring him back, remember this: Whoever turns a sinner from the error of his way will save him (*psychē*) from death and cover over a multitude of sins." (5:19-20)

Is he talking about physical death or eternal death? The context doesn't make it clear. A literal translation of verse 20, such as the NASB, reads: "... will save his soul (*psychē*) from death...." We evangelicals talk so much about "saving souls" that the phrase has become a technical term for us and it's difficult for us to hear it afresh. The word *psychē* is not a simple concept in the Greek language. It can mean "breath, earthly life" as well as carry the Greek ideas of the soul as the seat of the inner life of man that transcends the earthly. Usually, when we evangelicals use the word "soul," we use it in this Greek sense. The problem is that the corresponding Hebrew word *nephesh* doesn't really refer to the non-corporeal self, but to a person's essential "life,"[7] and this is the way that Hebrew speakers, such as James, would have used the term.

So does "death" to refer to physical death or eternal death? Paul warned the Corinthians that their sins at the Lord's Supper caused death: "This is why many among you are weak and sick, and a number of you have fallen asleep" (1 Corinthians 11:30). Earlier in Paul's letter he instructs the church how to treat open and blatant sin in their midst: "Hand this man over to Satan, so that the sinful nature (Greek *sarx*, KJV "flesh") may be destroyed and his spirit (*pneuma*) saved on the day of the Lord" (1 Corinthians 5:5)

So does James refer to spiritual death or physical death? Does he use the word *psychē*, "soul," to refer to that part of us that lives eternally or to our physical life breath? Does James really distinguish as carefully between "soul" and "spirit" as some evangelicals do? I'm not certain.

This is *not* the place, however, to give some pat doctrinal assurance of salvation. That's certainly not how James treated the problem of lapsed believers.

All I know is that I would sure hate to die away from God, alone, and bearing the weight of my own sins – no matter what faith I had professed earlier in my life. James is insistent that we don't kid ourselves. Faith without works is dead (2:26).

So Christians are called upon to pray earnestly for their wandering Christian friends, and bring them back to the Lord if they can.

Q4. (5:19-20) In the light of James' emphasis on active faith vs. dead faith (2:17), why is the role of finding and bringing back the wandering sheep so important?
http://www.joyfulheart.com/forums/index.php?act=ST&f=64&t=302

As James mentions wandering believers, my thoughts go to what Jesus says about wandering sheep. He tells a parable:

> "If a man owns a hundred sheep, and one of them wanders away, will he not leave the ninety-nine on the hills and go to look for the one that wandered off? And if he finds it, I tell you the truth, he is happier about that one sheep than about the ninety-nine that did not wander off. In the same way your Father in heaven is not willing that any of these little ones should be lost." (Matthew 18:12-14)

I can picture in my mind's eye Jesus the Good Shepherd out after dark, scouring the hills for that one sheep that is missing. He searches on one hill, and then in the valley

---

[7] See *psychē*, BAGD 893-894.

behind the hill. Always looking, gently calling the sheep by name – yes, shepherds knew each of their sheep by name. He searches relentlessly, and he calls again and again, and he doesn't give up until late into the night he finds that wandering sheep. And when he does, he is happy. He lifts that sheep over his shoulders and brings him back to the campfire and the sheepfold with joy and rejoicing, and invites the other shepherds to join him in a little celebration.

If you have a Christian friend who is wandering, then Jesus is your example of unremitting love. If you are the wandering sheep yourself, then remember that Jesus is still seeking you out. He is gently calling your name. He so much wants to bring you home. He wants so much to save your soul from death. He has died to cover your multitude of sins.

Won't you come home?

Won't you come home? He's still searching – for you!

Prayer

Lord, we thank you for an opportunity to catch a glimpse of your searching heart, searching for lost ones. Implant that bold prayer and tender seeking within me and within my brothers and sisters. And Lord, if one is reading this who is wandering alone, please find him or her, and gently bring them home. In Jesus' name I pray. Amen.

Key Verses

"Is any one of you sick? He should call the elders of the church to pray over him and anoint him with oil in the name of the Lord. And the prayer offered in faith will make the sick person well; the Lord will raise him up. If he has sinned, he will be forgiven. Therefore confess your sins to each other and pray for each other so that you may be healed. The prayer of a righteous man is powerful and effective." (5:14-16)

Appendix 1: Participant Guide Handout Sheets

This appendix provides copies of handouts designed for classes and small groups. There is no charge whatsoever to print out as many copies of the handouts as you need for participants.

www.jesuswalk.com/james/james-lesson-handouts.pdf

All notes are copyrighted and must bear the line:

You may not resell these notes to other groups or individuals outside your congregation. You may, however, charge people in your group enough to cover your copying costs.

Each of these lesson sheets includes:

Questions. You'll find 4 to 6 questions for each lesson. Each question may include several sub-questions. These are designed to get group members engaged in discussion of the key points of the passage. If you're running short of time, feel free to skip questions or portions of questions.

Key Verses. Each of these passages is rich in Bible verses worth memorizing. The verses here are in the New International Version, but feel free to have your members memorize in any translation you're comfortable with. Scripture memory has a way of fixing God's word in our minds. If you haven't tried assigning verses for memory – and then testing the following week – you'll bless your group members, though they may complain about short memories.

"I have hidden your word in my heart that I might not sin against you." (Psalm 119:11, NIV)

1. Experiencing Joy in Trials (1:1-18)
2. Hearing and Practicing the Word (1:18-27)
3. Forsaking Favoritism for Love (2:1-13)
4. Energizing Your Faith by Works (2:14-26)
5. Attaining Tongue-Taming Wisdom (3:1-18)
6. Submitting Yourself to God (4:1-12)
7. Learning Patience in an Instant Age (4:13-5:12)
8. Praying the Prayer of Faith (5:13-20)

1. Experiencing Joy in Trials (1:1-18)

Q1. (1:2-4) What value have trials had in your life? Have you let Satan destroy you with those trials? Or allowed God to refine you? How have you changed?

Q2. (1:13-15) Why do people blame God for evil? Does God tempt us with evil? Does he tempt sinful people with evil? Why does he allow people to sin? Why does he allow evil to exist at all?

Q3. (1:5-8) How do trials help cure us of "double mindedness"? How do trials help us grow in faith?

Q4. (1:5-8) What is the promise to claim in verse 5? What is the condition attached to this promise in verse 6? How do trials help us receive this wisdom?

Key Verses

"Consider it pure joy, my brothers, whenever you face trials of many kinds." (James 1:2)

"If any of you lacks wisdom, he should ask God, who gives generously to all without finding fault, and it will be given to him." (James 1:5)

"Every good and perfect gift is from above, coming down from the Father of the heavenly lights, who does not change like shifting shadows." (James 1:17)

2. Hearing and Practicing the Word (James 1:18-27)

Q1. (1:18) In what sense are we given spiritual birth by the "word of truth"? What does spiritual life have to do with the Word?

Q2. (1:22) Why are we so easily fooled into that *listening* to Bible teaching means that we are living out righteous lives? What is the nature of the self-deception?

Q3. What is this "perfect law" that James mentions? How would you define it? How does it relate to the "royal law" (2:8)? In what sense does it bring liberty?

Q4. (1:26-27) Why does James make taming the tongue and caring for the poor the prime tests of pure religion? Why not the quality of our quiet time or worship?

Key Verses

"My dear brothers, take note of this: Everyone should be quick to listen, slow to speak and slow to become angry, [20]for man's anger does not bring about the righteous life that God desires." (James 1:19-20)

"Do not merely listen to the word, and so deceive yourselves. Do what it says." (James 1:22)

"Religion that God our Father accepts as pure and faultless is this: to look after orphans and widows in their distress and to keep oneself from being polluted by the world." (James 1:27)

3. Forsaking Favoritism for Love (2:1-13)

Q1. (2:1-3) What kind of person or what kind of sinner do you tend to discriminate against? What kind of people are you (or your church) trying to make a good impression on?

Q2. (2:4) In what way does favoritism make one a judge? How does favoritism make one a judge with "evil thoughts"?

Q3. (2:9-11) Why does James refer to the Great Commandment as the "Royal Law"? How is it more "royal" than the Mosaic Law? How does showing favoritism toward a rich person break the "Royal Law" towards that rich person? How does it break the "Royal Law" in regard to a poor person?

Q4. (2:13b) In what way is showing regard towards the wealthy (2:2-3) a denial of mercy? Extra credit: Read Hosea 6:6; Matthew 5:7; and 9:13. In what way does mercy "triumph over" (NIV, RSV, NASB) or "rejoice against" (KJV) judgment? What does this mean?

Key Verses

"If you really keep the royal law found in Scripture, "Love your neighbor as yourself," you are doing right. But if you show favoritism, you sin and are convicted by the law as lawbreakers." (James 2:8-9)

"Mercy triumphs over judgment!" (James 2:13b)

4. Energizing Your Faith by Works (2:14-26)

Q1. (2:14-18) In what sense is faith dead if it is unaccompanied by action? In what sense might (if that were possible) it be alive?

Q2. (2:15-16) To what degree are we responsible for the poor and needy in the church community? How about our responsibility for those outside the church, in the community at large?

Q3. (2:18-19) What is the difference between the "belief" of a demon and the "belief" of a practicing Christian? The "belief" of a non-practicing Christian?

Q4. (2:20-26) How does James' point about the necessity of works jive with Paul's emphasis on salvation by grace without works (Ephesians 2:8-10)?

Key Verses

"Suppose a brother or sister is without clothes and daily food. If one of you says to him, 'Go, I wish you well; keep warm and well fed,' but does nothing about his physical needs, what good is it? In the same way, faith by itself, if it is not accompanied by action, is dead." (James 2:15-17)

"But someone will say, 'You have faith; I have deeds.' Show me your faith without deeds, and I will show you my faith by what I do. You believe that there is one God. Good! Even the demons believe that–and shudder." (James 2:18-19)

5. Attaining Tongue-Taming Wisdom (3:1-18)

Q1. (3:1-2) Why does James discourage people from aspiring to be teachers of the Word? Why is greater strictness appropriate? Should you set higher standards for your pastor than you do for yourself?

Q2. (3:7-8) Read Matthew 12:34 and 15:18. In light of these verses, why is the tongue untamable? What has to happen before it can be tamed?

Q3. (3:13-16) In what ways are "bitter envy" and selfish ambition (3:14) direct opposites of "humility" (3:13)? How does denial of "bitter envy" and "selfish ambition" prevent healing? How does boasting about these prevent healing?

Q4. (3:17-18) With what tool do peacemakers sow peace? Why does this produce a ripening crop of righteousness? In whom does this crop grow?

Key Verse

"Not many of you should presume to be teachers, my brothers, because you know that we who teach will be judged more strictly." (James 3:1)

6. Submitting Yourself to God (4:1-12)

Q1. (4:1-3) Is God against pleasure? What wrong in living to increase one's pleasure?

Q2. (4:4) Why does James refer to church members as "adulteresses"? What does the adultery consist of? Who is the aggrieved husband? What is wrong with friendship with the world?

Q3. (4:6-10) Verses 7-10 contain 10 different commands. Why are these actions so vital? In what way do they go against our nature? Which of these commands is most difficult for you?

Q4. (4:11-12) In what way does bad-mouthing a neighbor cause you to be a judge of the law? Why is it tempting to bad-mouth others, do you think?

Key Verses

"When you ask, you do not receive, because you ask with wrong motives, that you may spend what you get on your pleasures." (James 4:3)

"You adulterous people, don't you know that friendship with the world is hatred toward God? Anyone who chooses to be a friend of the world becomes an enemy of God." (James 4:4)

"But he gives us more grace. That is why Scripture says:
   'God opposes the proud
   but gives grace to the humble.'
Submit yourselves, then, to God. Resist the devil, and he will flee from you." (James 4:6-7)

"Humble yourselves before the Lord, and he will lift you up." (James 4:10)

7. Learning Patience in an Instant Age (4:13-5:12)

Q1. (4:13-16) What danger is James warning us about in verses 13-16? How can we be humble in our planning without being indecisive and wishy-washy?

Q2. (5:5-6) What is the spiritual danger of our demand for comfort and luxury? *Extra credit:* How might our demand for low-priced good and services cause us to (1) oppress our own employees or (2) cause workers in this country or abroad to be under paid or oppressed? How does all this relate to the need for patience?

Q3. (5:7-8) What can happen to us Christians if we lack the patience to eagerly expect Christ's return? Why is patience so vital?

Q4. (5:9) What does our grumbling and complaining say about us? About our faith? About our patience?

Key Verses

"Anyone, then, who knows the good he ought to do and doesn't do it, sins." (James 4:17)

"Be patient, then, brothers, until the Lord's coming." (James 5:7a)

"Above all, my brothers, do not swear – not by heaven or by earth or by anything else. Let your 'Yes' be yes, and your 'No,' no, or you will be condemned." (James 5:12b)

8. Praying the Prayer of Faith (5:13-20)

Q1. (5:13-14) According to verse 14, who is to initiate prayer for healing? Why is this important?

Q2. (5:14) What is the elders' role in prayer for the sick? What must be their spiritual qualifications for this ministry of prayer?

Q3. (5:14-16) In the healing prayer, what is the role of oil? What is the role of the prayer of faith? What is the role of faith? What is the role of confession of sins?

Q4. (5:19-20) In the light of James' emphasis on active faith vs. dead faith (2:17), why is the role of finding and bringing back the wandering sheep so important?

Key Verses

"Is any one of you sick? He should call the elders of the church to pray over him and anoint him with oil in the name of the Lord. And the prayer offered in faith will make the sick person well; the Lord will raise him up. If he has sinned, he will be forgiven. Therefore confess your sins to each other and pray for each other so that you may be healed. The prayer of a righteous man is powerful and effective." (5:14-16)

Appendix 2: Selected Passages on the Second Coming of Christ

We're not spending much time on the important topic of Jesus' Second Coming, since it is mentioned but twice in James, 7:7 and 7:8. However, if you've never explored this topic in the Bible, here are a number of passages on the topic. We have made no attempt to be exhaustive, only suggestive.

Matthew 16:27 "For the Son of Man is going to come in his Father's glory with his angels, and then he will reward each person according to what he has done."

Matthew 24:26-51 "So if anyone tells you, 'There he is, out in the desert,' do not go out; or, 'Here he is, in the inner rooms,' do not believe it. 27 For as lightning that comes from the east is visible even in the west, so will be the coming of the Son of Man. 28Wherever there is a carcass, there the vultures will gather.

29Immediately after the distress of those days
'the sun will be darkened,
and the moon will not give its light;
the stars will fall from the sky,
and the heavenly bodies will be shaken.'

30 At that time the sign of the Son of Man will appear in the sky, and all the nations of the earth will mourn. They will see the Son of Man coming on the clouds of the sky, with power and great glory. 31 And he will send his angels with a loud trumpet call, and they will gather his elect from the four winds, from one end of the heavens to the other.

32 Now learn this lesson from the fig tree: As soon as its twigs get tender and its leaves come out, you know that summer is near. 33 Even so, when you see all these things, you know that it is near, right at the door. 34 I tell you the truth, this generation will certainly not pass away until all these things have happened. 35 Heaven and earth will pass away, but my words will never pass away.

36 No one knows about that day or hour, not even the angels in heaven, nor the Son, but only the Father. 37 As it was in the days of Noah, so it will be at the coming of the Son of Man. 38 For in the days before the flood, people were eating and drinking, marrying and giving in marriage, up to the day Noah entered the ark; 39 and they knew nothing about what would happen until the flood came and took them all away. That is how it will be at the coming of the Son of Man. 40 Two men will be in the field; one will be taken and the other left. 41 Two women will be grinding with a hand mill; one will be taken and the other left.

[42] Therefore keep watch, because you do not know on what day your Lord will come. [43] But understand this: If the owner of the house had known at what time of night the thief was coming, he would have kept watch and would not have let his house be broken into. [44] So you also must be ready, because the Son of Man will come at an hour when you do not expect him.

[45] Who then is the faithful and wise servant, whom the master has put in charge of the servants in his household to give them their food at the proper time? [46] It will be good for that servant whose master finds him doing so when he returns. [47] I tell you the truth, he will put him in charge of all his possessions. [48] But suppose that servant is wicked and says to himself, 'My master is staying away a long time,' [49] and he then begins to beat his fellow servants and to eat and drink with drunkards. [50] The master of that servant will come on a day when he does not expect him and at an hour he is not aware of. [51] He will cut him to pieces and assign him a place with the hypocrites, where there will be weeping and gnashing of teeth."

When the Son of Man comes in his glory, and all the angels with him, he will sit on his throne in heavenly glory. All the nations will be gathered before him, and he will separate the people one from another as a shepherd separates the sheep from the goats."

Matthew 25:31-32 "No one knows about that day or hour, not even the angels in heaven, nor the Son, but only the Father. Be on guard! Be alert! You do not know when that time will come. It's like a man going away: He leaves his house and puts his servants in charge, each with his assigned task, and tells the one at the door to keep watch."

Mark 13:32-37 "Therefore keep watch because you do not know when the owner of the house will come back–whether in the evening, or at midnight, or when the rooster crows, or at dawn. If he comes suddenly, do not let him find you sleeping. What I say to you, I say to everyone: 'Watch!'"

John 14:3 "And if I go and prepare a place for you, I will come back and take you to be with me that you also may be where I am."

Acts 1:11 "'Men of Galilee,' they said, 'why do you stand here looking into the sky? This same Jesus, who has been taken from you into heaven, will come back in the same way you have seen him go into heaven.'"

Philippians 3:20-21 "But our citizenship is in heaven. And we eagerly await a Savior from there, the Lord Jesus Christ, who, by the power that enables him to bring everything under his control, will transform our lowly bodies so that they will be like his glorious body."

1 Thessalonians 4:13-18 "Brothers, we do not want you to be ignorant about those who fall asleep, or to grieve like the rest of men, who have no hope. We believe that Jesus died and rose again and so we believe that God will bring with Jesus those who have fallen asleep in him. According to the Lord's own word, we tell you that we who are still alive, who are left till the coming of the Lord, will certainly not precede those who have fallen asleep. For the Lord himself will come down from heaven, with a loud command, with the voice of the archangel and with the trumpet call of God, and the dead in Christ will rise first. After that, we who are still alive and are left will be caught up together with them in the clouds to meet the Lord in the air. And so we will be with the Lord forever. Therefore encourage each other with these words."

1 Thessalonians 5:2 "... For you know very well that the day of the Lord will come like a thief in the night."

1 Thessalonians 5:23 "May God himself, the God of peace, sanctify you through and through. May your whole spirit, soul and body be kept blameless at the coming of our Lord Jesus Christ."

1 Timothy 6:14 ".... To keep this command without spot or blame until the appearing of our Lord Jesus Christ...."

2 Timothy 4:1 "In the presence of God and of Christ Jesus, who will judge the living and the dead, and in view of his appearing and his kingdom, I give you this charge."

Titus 2:13 "... While we wait for the blessed hope – the glorious appearing of our great God and Savior, Jesus Christ."

Hebrews 9:28 "... So Christ was sacrificed once to take away the sins of many people; and he will appear a second time, not to bear sin, but to bring salvation to those who are waiting for him."

Revelation 1:7 "Look, he is coming with the clouds,
and every eye will see him,
even those who pierced him;
and all the peoples of the earth will mourn because of him.
So shall it be! Amen."

Revelation 22:20 "He who testifies to these things says, 'Yes, I am coming soon.' Amen. Come, Lord Jesus."

Appendix 3. Other Resources on James

I've prepared two other resources on James that may interest you, but I didn't include them in this book in order to keep the price as low as possible. However, you may print them out from my website at no additional charge.

Inductive Bible Study Questions

www.jesuswalk.com/james/james-inductive-bible-study-questions.pdf

These questions are designed for groups that want to pull their learning entirely from the text. You are free to print these out for use with your congregation. There are three levels of questions for each lesson:

1. Observation Questions. What Does the Text Say?

2. Interpretation Questions. What Does the Text Mean?

3. Application Questions. What Does It Mean to Me?

Readers' Theater Scripts

www.jesuswalk.com/james/james-readers-theater.pdf

These are scripts based on the NIV, typically designed for three readers, that provide emphasis at key points to bring out the meaning of the text. My goal has been that when the group or congregation hears the scripture read in this way, the main points will stick and they will be better prepared for the sermon or Bible study. You are free to print these out for use with your group or congregation.

CPSIA information can be obtained at www.ICGtesting.com
Printed in the USA
BVOW040756100413

317776BV00006B/195/P